D0102005

MELBOURNE
THEN & NOW

MELBOURNE
THEN & NOW

HEATHER CHAPMAN & JUDITH STILLMAN

THUNDER BAY
P·R·E·S·S

San Diego, California

Thunder Bay Press
An imprint of the Advantage Publishers Group
5880 Oberlin Drive, San Diego, CA 92121-4794
www.thunderbaybooks.com

Produced by PRC Publishing
151 Freston Road
London W10 6TH, United Kingdom

An imprint of Anova Books Company Ltd

© 2005 PRC Publishing

Copyright under International, Pan American, and Universal Copyright Conventions.
All rights reserved. No part of this book may be reproduced or transmitted in any form
or by any means, electronic or mechanical, including photocopying, recording, or by any
information storage-and-retrieval system, without written permission from the copyright
holder. Brief passages (not to exceed 1,000 words) may be quoted for reviews.

All notations of errors or omissions should be addressed to Thunder Bay Press,
Editorial Department, at the above address. All other correspondence (author
inquiries, permissions) concerning the content of this book should be addressed to
PRC Publishing, 151 Freston Road, London W10 6TH, United
Kingdom. An imprint of Anova Books Company Ltd.

ISBN 1 59223 552 2

Printed and bound in China

2 3 4 5 09 08 07 06 05

Acknowledgements:

We gratefully acknowledge the assistance of the following:
Staff of the La Trobe Reading Room, State Library of Victoria, Dianne Temby (Master of Museum
Studies), Penny Irons (Lecturer of Tourism, William Angliss Institute; PTGAA), Steve and Robin Street
(ImageStreet Historical Photos), Bill Meares (Secretary Brighton Bathing Box Association Inc.).

Thanks also to:
The Dean of St. Paul's Cathedral, The Very Reverend David Richardson and Verger Peter Dwyer, Louise
Kinder (Executive Assistant to the Governor of Victoria), Robynne Danks (Worley Parsons Engineering)
Shane Brown (MCC Communications), Adrian Dent (Grand Hotel), Clara Nunez (Lend Lease-
Docklands)

Picture Credits:

The publisher wishes to thank the following for kindly supplying the photographs that appear in this book:

Then photographs:
© Hulton-Deutsch Collection/CORBIS: 14.
Image Street Heritage Photos of Australia: 1, 20, 44, 64, 74, 106, 114, 126, 130.
LaTrobe Picture Collection, State Library of Victoria: 6, 8, 10, 12, 16, 18, 22, 24, 26, 28, 30, 32, 34, 36,
38, 40, 42, 46, 48, 52, 54, 56, 58, 60, 62, 66, 68, 70, 72, 76, 78, 80, 82, 84, 86, 88, 90, 92, 94, 96, 98, 100,
102, 104, 108, 110, 112, 116, 120, 122, 124, 128, 132, 136, 138, 140, 142.
LaTrobe Picture Collection, State Library of Victoria / © Rose Stereograph Co: 118.
© Clements Langford Pty Ltd Collection, University of Melbourne Archives, Image ID UMA/I/2430: 50.

Now photographs:
All photographs were taken by Simon Clay (© Anova Image Library).

Anova Books Company Ltd. is committed to respecting the intellectual property rights of others. We have
therefore taken all reasonable efforts to ensure that the reproduction of all content on these pages is done
with the full consent of copyright owners. If you are aware of any unintentional omissions please contact
the company directly so that any necessary corrections may be made for future editions.

INTRODUCTION

"This will be the place for a village," declared John Batman when in 1835 he found, six miles up the Yarra, good deep water and gently sloping wooded land suitable for settlement and his pastoral interests. Others before him had not stayed but Batman negotiated with the local aboriginals exchanging looking glasses, scissors, clothing and blankets for land. At the same time, John Pascoe Fawkner was also engaged in finding more pastoral land. These squatters on Crown land began the fledgling unauthorised European settlement called Bearbrass.

Authorities in New South Wales were infuriated by the rogue settlement but Governor Bourke, the administrator responsible for the colonies, bowed to the inevitable and legitimised the Port Phillip settlement in 1837. By this time there were about 100 houses clustered around the port area on the river. Surveyor Robert Hoddle drew up the plans for the new city to be called Melbourne after the Prime Minister of England. It was never a haphazard settlement but rather a carefully-planned city. Hoddle's rectangular grid had 32 x 10-acre blocks that began at the river. The streets of the Hoddle Grid were to be 30 metres (99 feet) wide and 200 metres (660 feet) apart. Large areas of land around this were set aside for Government use and for parks and gardens. By 1842 there were more than 1000 buildings and all the major urban functions were in place.

The state of Victoria was proclaimed in 1851. There were more than 80,000, mainly British people living in Victoria and of these, 20,000 were in Melbourne. Gold changed everything. In 1851 the discovery of the largest gold nugget the world had ever seen led to the Victorian Gold Rush. Melbourne's population grew seven-fold in a decade. British, Europeans, Californians, Irish and Chinese flocked to Melbourne bringing with them new skills and lifestyles, egalitarian attitudes and radical ideas such as Unionism, "a fair day's work for a fair day's pay" and the right for women to vote. Over the next ten years the Victorian goldfields produced one third of the world's gold and by 1885 this wealth brought to Melbourne such a building boom and such optimism that the city became known as "Marvellous Melbourne". Dynamic entrepreneurs like Frederick Sargood built grand, elegant homes, stores, industrial enterprises and public buildings. Melbourne wanted to show the world how wealthy, grand and civilised she was and it is at this time that some of the great classical buildings, Parliament House, Exhibition Building and St. Patrick's Cathedral, were constructed. Gold funded the important institutions like Melbourne University, The National Gallery and the National Museum. Even today Melbourne is considered the cultural capital of the nation.

And then came the collapse. Over-speculation in land followed by rural drought lead to the Depression of the 1890s. Banks and many small companies closed, thousands of people lost their jobs and savings, and almost no new buildings were erected until 1900.

The new century ushered in the Federation of Australia with Melbourne as its capital until 1927. Electricity transformed the city. Electric street lighting, electric trams, theatres and cinemas, like the State Theatre, dramatically increased the numbers of people coming into the central business district for work and leisure. Building resumed but restrictions were now imposed. A fear of congestion and the model of Paris as a well-planned city, led to the setting of height limits. Overall, a uniform profile prevailed but new reinforced concrete buildings began to dominate the skyline that was once the province of spires and domes.

The two world wars and the intervening Depression changed Melbourne once more. Thousands of Melburnians had enlisted and many lost their lives in foreign countries. Women had to enter the workforce in large numbers and developed skills in many new areas. A shortage of labour and building materials meant that there were comparatively few new buildings constructed. Exceptions were the wonderful Art Deco buildings, Manchester Unity, Myers, G.J. Coles and Russell Street Police Headquarters.

Melbourne's cultural diversity also changed after the war. British immigrants came but thousands of others too, from Yugoslavia, Germany, the Netherlands and Malta. Many arrived as "assisted migrants", passages paid for by the Australian Government. Immigrants from Greece and Italy in the 1950s and 1960s joined those who had come earlier in the century. The 1970s and 1980s also brought Asian migrants to Melbourne. As in previous times, Melbourne benefited from the new ideas, energy and optimism of the newcomers.

The post-war glass and steel high-rise buildings changed Melbourne's skyline forever. In the mid 1970s there had been a very strong public voice to protect fine city buildings like the Windsor hotel, and streetscapes such as Collins Street. Although some were demolished, Melbourne today is one of the few cities to have retained much of its original Victorian architecture. By the twenty-first century, towers in excess of 50 storeys were appearing around the fringe of the retail centre.

Shopping in the retail core declined during the 1970s as large one-stop shopping centres and malls developed in the suburbs. This trend was reversed during the mid-1980s when residential apartments that included supermarkets, improved public transport, and entertainment areas brought people into the city once more. People now sat under umbrellas and leafy trees at footpath cafés. In 1990 there were only 1000 bars and cafés in central Melbourne but by 2002 there were 18,000.

Batman's decision that this would be "the place for a village" proved to be fortuitous. Melbourne is ideally sited; its position at the head of a deeply indented bay places it almost in the centre of its region. In the first 50 years of European settlement, the patterns of Melbourne's future development were set, patterns recognisable in the twenty-first century. Today, more than 160 different nationalities make up Melbourne's population of 3.8 million.

Flinders Street Station, the grand redbrick and golden-stucco building stretching for two city blocks, dominates this corner of Melbourne. The original railway building was a collection of wooden sheds where the first mechanical rail journey in Australia was made in 1854. When a new viaduct linked this station with Spencer Street Station the smaller station could not cope. A competition was held for a new building and Fawcett and Ashworth won the prize of £500. Building commenced in 1901 and was completed in 1910. It included a huge dome, arched entrance, a clock tower, ballroom, library, concert hall, meeting rooms and a crèche where you could leave your children for two shillings a day. This Edwardian baroque building looked so different that some believed it was really meant for Bombay. In 1910 Flinders Street Station claimed to be the busiest station in the world.

"I'll meet you under the clocks" has only one meaning for all Victorians. Flinders Street Station has been both a transit and meeting place throughout its history, the steps under the clocks crowded with those coming, going and waiting. When the analogue clocks showing the departure times for each suburban line were replaced with digital clocks, there was an immediate outcry and the original clocks quickly reappeared overhead. Flinders Street Station is the hub of an extensive rail network and each work day more than 110,000 commuters walk through its turnstiles making it the busiest suburban rail station in Australia. Platform No. 1, at 708 metres (2,323 feet), is the longest in Australia and the fourth longest in the world. Renovation is ongoing and includes new lifts, escalators, tactile-tiled platforms and attractive open concourses.

Swanston Street is the spine of the city and the route down which parades move. It became the most important thoroughfare in Melbourne with the opening of the Princes Bridge in 1851, the route to St. Kilda Road and the south-eastern suburbs. During World War II, Australia had a population of just over seven million. In a spirit of great patriotism and with the overwhelming agreement of the people, 993,000 young men and women left to go to war. Large parades were held, such as this one up Swanston Street past St. Paul's Cathedral, the Victoria Building and the Town Hall where dignitaries wished the troops safe passage and where banners urged people to buy war bonds. People lined the streets to show their support. Australians felt a great allegiance to Britain and, like New Zealand, immediately took up arms in defence of the "mother country" and to fight the Japanese in the Pacific theatre of war. Life changed forever in Australia as more women entered the workforce to do the jobs previously done by men. Shortages of goods were common and rationing was introduced.

In this street are some of the city's most important public buildings: the Town Hall, the State Library, St. Paul's Cathedral and until recently, the former Queen Victoria Hospital. The Victoria Buildings near the Town Hall were demolished in 1960. The Melbourne Town Hall, located here in the geographical heart of the city, is the seat of Local Government. The present building, designed by Joseph Reed, was erected between 1884 and 1886, its impressive exterior a testament to the wealth and pride of the city. In 1991 the City of Melbourne closed Swanston Street to general traffic to make it more pedestrian friendly but this was not universally accepted so it was reopened to general evening traffic in 1999.

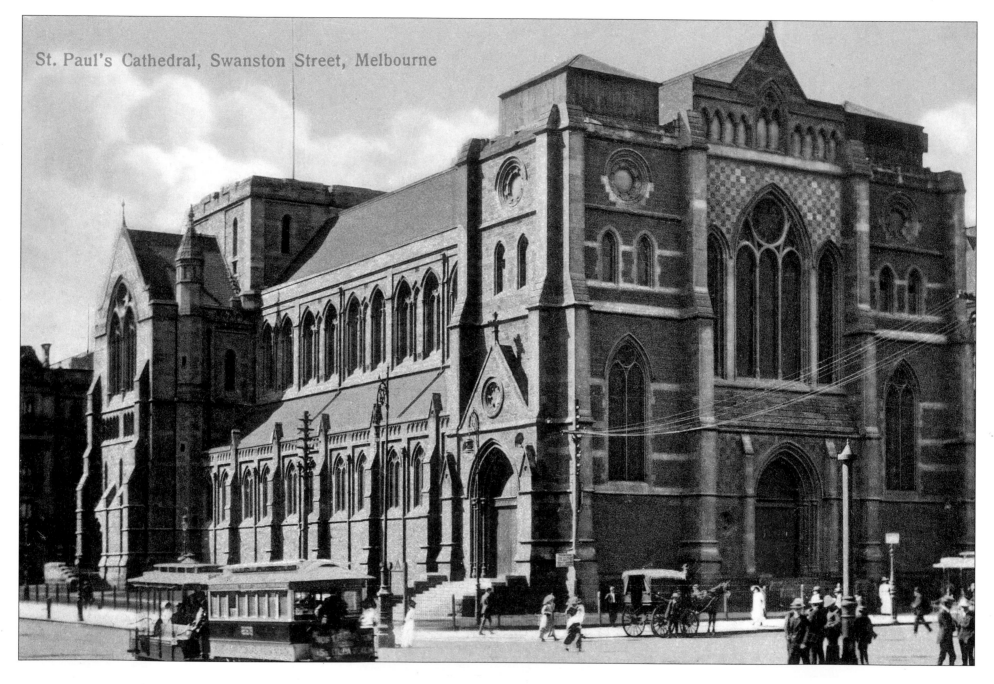

St. Paul's Cathedral, Swanston Street, Melbourne

In 1836, public Christian services on this site were held under a gum tree. Between 1841 and 1848 this area became a corn market. When the new Eastern Market was opened, the merchants moved there and the site became vacant. St. James in the west could no longer accommodate all the worshippers so a new church was required. Charles and James Webb designed the new church that was consecrated in 1852. This was replaced between 1880 and 1891 by a much grander sandstone building designed by William Butterfield, a noted English architect. Butterfield never saw the building and resigned after frequent arguments with the church authorities in Australia. Joseph Reed completed the cathedral, the tallest building in Melbourne at that time. The interior was filled with light through the many spectacular stained glass windows.

In 1926 the architect Joseph Reed added the spires we see today. They are made from different stone and appear darker than other parts of the building. Although St. Paul's is still a striking feature of this site and its spires a recognisable landmark, the rise of many taller twentieth-century buildings around has robbed it of its dominance of the city skyline. Many feared that the plans for the new Federation Square buildings would block the view of the cathedral from the south because the original plans showed glass shards positioned in the corner opposite the cathedral. Protests were voiced throughout the media, and politicians lobbied until a compromise was reached with the architects that ensured that the view from the south was not obscured. It has actually been enhanced and the cathedral is now open to Flinders Street and the Square in a new way.

John Batman, who had already built a house on this site, bought the land at the first land auctions in 1837. When he died it became the first schoolhouse in the new colony. By 1842, Melbourne's population had grown to over 10,000 and this central site was so valuable that it was subdivided and five bluestone warehouses and a butcher's shop were erected. Two successful Irishmen bought the buildings in 1875 and the five separate buildings became Young and Jackson's Princes Bridge Hotel, a place of "stale beer, tobacco and choice language" according to *The Argus* newspaper. There was no love lost between the hotel patrons and those of the cathedral opposite but, during "the Great Fire" in Flinders Street in 1897, the publican was able to save his barrels by rolling them across to the cathedral. Melbourne's puritans were even more scandalized when a nude painting, "Chloe", appeared in the public bar.

Situated at the busiest intersection in Melbourne, Young and Jackson's was a favourite meeting place for young soldiers and sailors. Through four wars, servicemen toasted "Chloe" and even wrote letters to her from the Front. In the 1960s, young people gained a rare opportunity to see a nude female body. The long-standing 6pm closing time for hotels, between 1915 and 1966, led to the workers rushing to "swill" many pots of beer in a short time, spilling out of the pub and staggering homeward bound across the road to crowded trams and trains. Today, the renovated hotel is no longer a place of "bad smells and choice language" and is an attractive place to meet friends. "Chloe" has moved upstairs and Heritage Victoria decreed in 1988 that she and Young & Jackson's remain together forever.

Collins Street was the elite street in Melbourne. The western end was the financial heart of the city, its eastern end the preserve of the wealthy from the earliest days. Here were the homes and businesses of doctors, dentists, businessmen and pastoralists whose wives shopped in the exclusive stores like Georges near the Town Hall or in the fashionable boutiques of The Block closer to Elizabeth Street. To "do the Block" was to promenade late in the afternoon or on Saturday morning waiting to be seen by the people who mattered. The Manchester Unity Building, completed in 1932, was taller than the Town Hall but the Town Hall was still the more prominent, reflecting the civic pride of the city. The clock tower was named after the Duke of Edinburgh on the occasion of his second visit to Melbourne in 1867.

Collins Street remains Melbourne's most exclusive street. Georges department store, a Melbourne institution, has closed to the regret of Melburnians—even those who couldn't afford to shop there. The eastern end still has exclusive shops, doctors' and dentists' surgeries but its reputation as the "Paris end of Collins Street" has been dented. High-rise hotels and office buildings were allowed to sprout there before public outrage was noted. Collins Street has been tree-lined since the members of the Melbourne Club talked the City Council into planting them in 1875. The corner where the Town Hall and the Manchester Unity Building stand is still one of Melbourne's busiest intersections, the Town Hall steps rather than the Manchester Unity Building being the place to meet friends. The Block further west from the corner is still a charming and elegant place to shop. It is strange that today the expression to "do the Block" means to lose one's temper.

In 1835 John Batman's party had sailed up both the Maribyrnong and Yarra Rivers but it was here, 9.7 Kilometres (6 miles) upstream, where the water was deep and wide enough for ships to dock and turn, that the new settlement grew. Fresh water was plentiful. A reef of rocks prevented the tidal water from flowing upstream; the falls created by these rocks were called "yarro yarro" or "yarra yarra", by the local Aborigines. Queen's Wharf became

the commercial area of the settlement and a Customs House, warehouses, a market square and hotels developed around here. On the southern bank factories were built, as they too needed port access. The viaduct linking the railway stations of Flinders Street and Spencer Street was opened in 1891. Beneath this viaduct, part of the Flinders Street Station building complex, were vaults where merchants from the Western Market stored their fruit.

When the Victoria Docks were built towards the end of the nineteenth century and a new bridge was constructed downstream at Spencer Street in 1930, the Queen's Wharf docks became obsolete and the surrounding businesses lost their locational advantage. The area fell into decline. This part of the city became shabby and neglected. The situation worsened with the raising of Flinders Street in 1961 to allow for the new Kingsway work and businesses suffered as public access to their premises became more and more difficult. A hotel closed soon after the opening of the new overpass and empty derelict shops remained on the market for years—a perfect example of urban blight. Various government plans have come to little over the years but the latest, to remove the overpass by 2006, looks more promising. Many hope that the north bank will then reflect the prosperity of the casino opposite.

The collection of customs duties on all incoming and outgoing goods provided the main source of revenue in the early days of the colony. It was natural that the Customs House be located as close as possible to the point of entry, Queen's Wharf. The Immigration Department was further west near the Fish Market. The original Customs House was bought from John Pascoe Fawkner, one of the founders of Melbourne, in 1837 for £100. During the

1850s gold brought thousands of people and a new Customs House was needed to process them. Construction took 25 years because the goldrushes had caused a labour shortage. The customs officers had to censor written materials, making sure that they conformed to the social values of the time, and to administer the Immigration Preservation Act of 1901 that, through a dictation test, preserved the white English-speaking base of the population.

The Customs House, as well as fulfilling its expected customs role, was also the place where waterfront workers applied for their licences to work. In the late 1920s it was the scene of fierce industrial riots as stevedores and coal-handlers, on strike for improved conditions, fought with non-union labour. The "wharfies" armed themselves with rotten vegetables and fruit from the nearby Western Market and pelted the strike-breakers. The riot spread to nearby city streets and one man was killed when the police fired into the crowd. Eventually the wharfies were forced to return to work, re-applying for their licences at the Customs House. In recent years the Customs House has served other purposes, even providing a temporary home for politicians who couldn't be accommodated in the area around parliament. Today it is home to the Museum of Hellenic Antiquities and the Immigration Museum.

The Fish Market was built in 1890 and operated between 1892 and 1959. This wonderfully ornate red and white building, with its clock tower and copper turrets, covered 5.7 acres, squeezed between Flinders Street and the railway viaduct. The viaduct and the cool stores separated it from the river but it was still well located, close to the wharves and the nearby Western Market. The fish arrived at Little Dock on the other side of Spencer Street, and was then transported on noisy little trolleys to the Fish Market, and from there to the Western Market nearby. At the time, the market was supposed to have the latest ideas in food handling but the hawkers, who distributed the fish around the streets of the city, ignored the inspectors and much bad seafood caused grief to the unwitting public. Shopkeepers complained often to the papers and politicians about the smells and the bad language used by these hawkers.

In 1958, the need to build a second rail viaduct meant that the Fish Market was demolished, despite great public outrage. Many still consider this an act of vandalism. The busy fish markets were moved to new premises at Footscray, outside the central city area. Now the area is a hotch-potch of rail lines, tramlines, overhead wires, boarded-up buildings and a car park from which the City Council nets $1 million per year. The 1961 King Street alterations added to the decline as local vehicular and pedestrian needs gave way to the demands of through traffic. Now the entire area along the north bank of the Yarra is marked for urban renewal, some of which is to be completed by 2006. The lawn area marks where the government cool stores stood and the buildings to the right of the Yarra River are part of the casino.

Railway Offices, Spencer Street.

The Administrative Building of the Victorian Railways Department was the largest building to be built in Melbourne in the nineteenth century. The site had previously been the first racetrack and then became part of Batman's land. When Batman died in 1839 his cottage became available for use by the Railways' Department. By the 1880s, the current buildings were inadequate and William Greene drew up plans for a grand office building. It was constructed in the Italian style, of brick, concrete and stucco, three storeys high. Its Spencer Street frontage was 119 metres (130 yards) wide, and its 300 rooms accommodated 1,200 employees. Statues adorned the upper levels, but these were eventually removed when they began to crumble and fall on pedestrians below. The building was grand rather than beautiful—a monument to the importance of rail.

Between 1912 and 1922 the Railway Building was extended and another floor and attics were added where once ornamentation and parapet had been. Since that time the building has been further altered. It continued to be the head office of the railways until 1985 when the Ministry of Transport and V-Line administration moved to a tower in Collins Street. In 1988, at the height of the property boom, the building was sold to joint partners. When property market prices plummeted it was again sold, this time to a hotel chain. Since 1997 it has been extensively renovated, the architects maintaining the grandeur wherever possible. The central staircase has been fully restored and the ceilings on Level 5 display the unique concave iron of the original building. The Grand Central Apartments occupy the northern end and the Grand Hotel at the southern end offers 4-Star accommodation.

The Griffiths Brothers name goes back to 1879. They were one of the first tea, coffee and cocoa distribution companies in Australia. In 1900, the Griffiths Tea Building in Flinders Street was commissioned and it was to be Romanesque in style, similar to other warehouses in Flinders Street. This redbrick building with its cream stucco bands and tall arched windows was their new store and sales room. The Griffiths Brothers were canny marketers. Recognizing the importance of rail travel they used the system to advertise their products. On rail sidings and fences all over Australia their distinctive blue and white enamel signs could be seen proclaiming the distance in miles to the next cup of Griffiths tea. During the 1920s the Herald newspaper group, already occupying most of the eastern part of Flinders Street, took over the building.

In the 1940s, the Griffiths Building was renamed "Gravure House" and was the home of such publications as *Home Beautiful* and *Your Garden*. Between 1973 and 1988 the building was leased as a billiard and snooker centre by a member of the famous Lindrum family. This family produced four generations of champion billiard and snooker players. Walter Lindrum, the best known of them, rewrote the record books and claimed 57 billiards world records. Lindrums' occupation of the building ended when News Limited (Rupert Murdoch's media group) occupied the premises as offices for *The Australian* newspaper. In 1995 David Marriner, a developer interested in preserving Melbourne's history, took over, and it was opened as the boutique Hotel Lindrum. In the billiard room visitors can play on one of the original Alcock billiard tables and view the Walter Lindrum memorabilia.

Surveyor Hoddle had planned that there should be narrow streets, 10 metres (33 feet) wide, for the delivery of goods to the businesses of the main streets of Melbourne. Drays could enter the rear of the premises without interrupting the movement of people and carriages on the main streets. However, from the earliest years, the lanes were much more than conduits. Warehouses built there because of the cheaper cost of land, shared the lanes with workers'

cottages, pig pens, and cowsheds. By the twentieth century, Melbourne was a great commercial city and the laneways had become essential pathways for people and industry. Subdivisions had created even more alleys and laneways. Each lane had its distinctive character and the eastern part of Flinders Lane, close to Swanston Street, was the home of the rag trade and its associated industries, pleating, sewing-machine repairs and leatherwork.

Melbourne is the home of Australia's fashion industry and Flinders Lane is still its centre. Here you will find, hidden from public notice, a simple brass plaque that announces the name of a famous fashion design house. If you can afford the designs then you know the location. They do not need to advertise. Some of the larger businesses, requiring cheaper and more spacious facilities, have moved out of the Central Business District to nearby suburbs from where they draw their labour supply. The manufacturers of footwear, bags and belts, men and women's clothing have gone. Tertiary educational institutions, hotels and commercial enterprises now use the former textile premises. At street-level shops, art galleries, and cafés have moved in. Flinders Lane has long been a one-way street but it remains one of the most congested in the city.

People could drown in Elizabeth Street in its early days, as it was a natural watercourse, originally called Williams Creek, that became impassable after heavy rain. Drays vanished, horses, drivers and cattle drowned. Drainage began in 1841 but even in 1900, after heavy rains, both Elizabeth and Swanston Streets were impassable, dividing the east and west sides of the town. The wide street allowed carriage and horse teams to turn easily without interference from the cable trams that terminated close to Flinders Street Station. Elegant awnings marked the entrances to stores such as Craig Williamson (right). On the left is the Australian Building which in 1888 was the third highest building in the world. Shops allied to the textile trade, barristers, banks, cafes and oyster bars crowded this busy end of the street. At its northern end it became the main route to the goldfields.

This intersection remains one of the busiest spots in the city. In the foreground most of the grand old shops have either been demolished or given a utilitarian facelift. Newsagents, chemists, tobacconists, and supermarkets fulfil the needs of rushed workers. The modern tram terminus gives protection to workers as they wait to be transported to the Victoria markets, Flemington racecourse, major hospitals and the northern suburbs. The grand Australian Building, demolished in 1980, has been replaced by a structure of cement and glass, as have so many others. On the Collins Street corner (right), at the start of the Block, is the site of the first brick building in Melbourne, Brunton's Building. This Edwardian brick and cream building, with its turret and decorative balconies, so dominant in the early twentieth century streetscape, is a barely visible reminder of past times.

Stewart Dawson's store on the corner of Swanston and Collins Streets had been a trysting place for many years, so in 1928, when it was sold to the Independent Order of Oddfellows, there was an immediate outcry. This did not last long. Melburnians watched in amazement as the city's tallest building began to take shape. The Manchester Unity Building was erected in record time between 1929 and 1932 at the height of the Depression, using round-the-clock labour. This 12-storey Art Deco building was modelled on the Chicago Tribune Building. Its dramatic ribbing extended to a tower higher than the then height limit of 132 feet, possible because the tower was uninhabited. Inside the building there was an arcade and the walls were faced in marble. On the walls there were sculptural depictions of people engaged in worthy activities. The building was the first one to have a rooftop café, a pond, palm trees and an aviary full of exotic birds.

The Manchester Unity Building is often voted Melburnians' favourite building, its vertical lines just as pleasing to the eye as they were in 1932. The marble that lines the interior, the marquetry, bevelled glass, brass and copper is wonderfully preserved. Of course it is on one of the city's busiest corners, far too busy to be used for a meeting place, but it also remains deep in the subconscious mind of every little girl who ever rattled past in a tram in earlier times. Then the large first floor windows displayed bridal and evening gowns, little girls' dreams come true. Today diamond merchants, wholesale jewellers, and goldsmiths occupy these upper floors, perhaps the things bigger girls dream about. Dentists and other professionals also have rooms here. The tower is now an apartment.

The Alexandra Theatre, named after Alexandra, wife of the future King Edward VII, opened its doors in 1886 with a production of a farcical comedy *Bad Lads*. In 1891, the production of Fenimore Cooper's *The Scout* caused a sensation. A huge tank of water was the centrepiece. Over 100,000 people in a six-week season watched in amazement as the actors performed on horseback and in the water. Melbourne already had many live theatres but this one was crucial in the development of live theatre in Australia. Here J.C. Williamson began his long career fostering the dramatic arts. Australians had very strong ties to England and he renamed the theatre Her Majesty's in 1900 in honour of Queen Victoria. It is ironic that a staunchly anti-royalist organization like The Anarchist Club had made its home there between 1886 and 1890.

Dame Nellie Melba, Dame Margot Fonteyn, Anna Pavlova and Dame Joan Sutherland have all performed here at Her Majesty's. This is where Dame Nellie Melba gave her farewell performance. The Borovansky Ballet, the forerunner of the Australian Ballet, was based here for 17 years. The great twentieth century Broadway musicals, Gilbert and Sullivan hits, grand opera, and Shakespearean drama have all been performed at this venue. Over time Her Majesty's has had change forced upon it. A disastrous fire in 1929 almost destroyed it and the auditorium had to be completely rebuilt. Modern theatrical productions demand large areas both on stage and off, and since new owners took over in 2000, Her Majesty's has again been refurbished.

The Congregationalist chapel in the new colony, built on the corner of Collins and Russell Streets, was completed in 1841 and originally called the Collins Street Independent Church. Prior to this, services had been held in John Pascoe Fawkner's tavern. The parishioners were mainly farmers and farm workers. The chapel was demolished in 1866 and Joseph Reed designed this new church in the style of the medieval Italian churches with polychrome brickwork, open cloisters and Romanesque arches. The interior was very different from the traditional arrangement of pews and pulpit. The tiered seating was arranged on a sloping floor, and a gallery was built to increase the capacity of the church. Seating was in a semi-circular pattern so that the entire congregation could see, hear, and be close to the preacher. The stained glass windows date from 1869 and are considered unique. The Burke and Wills monument, at this intersection from 1865 to 1886, was a constant hazard for traffic.

Today St. Michael's Uniting Church is well known as a centre of liberal progressive theology, and as a provider of counselling and psychotherapy services. In the 1970s the church was renovated, the interior was remodelled, the organ and choir were relocated, new pews were installed, and the chancel was raised to highlight the Cross and Communion table. In 1977 the Methodists, Congregationalists, and most of the Presbyterians combined to form the Uniting Church. In 1990 it was again renamed, this time more accurately, St. Michael's Uniting Church. In 1988, on the occasion of the 150th anniversary of the church and Australia's Bicentenary, modern stained glass windows by artist Klaus Zimmer were installed. In 1999, the sanctuary Mingary was opened, a place for quiet contemplation in the middle of a busy city. Throughout the week some of Melbourne's best musicians perform here and can be enjoyed by all.

Cyclorama, a novel form of entertainment, opened in October 1891. It was a large, circular building with scenes depicting important events painted on the interior walls. Real trees, sand, other props, back-lighting, sound effects and a running commentary were used to make the scene come alive. The audience stood on a central platform to watch "The Siege of Paris" (the Franco-Prussian War) or "The Battle of Waterloo" unfold. This was a sort of 3D documentary in the round in the days before cinema. It attracted large crowds when it first opened but unfortunately the economic downturn of the 1890s meant that few could afford this entertainment. Cyclorama closed in 1894.

Following its closure, the Little Collins Street Cyclorama was converted to warehouses. The building was remodelled in 1901, then again in the 1950s and the 1960s. It became the Hostess Store for the exclusive Georges Store of Collins Street. When Georges was no longer an economically viable business the building was again remodelled and became The Georges Apartments in 1995. A mansard roof was added and the curved glass shop fronts gave it a

Parisian style. Some of the windows of the earlier structure can be seen, installed above the entrance foyer. Quists Coffee Shop, Melbourne's first coffee roaster, has been at this location since 1938. Coffee used to be roasted in the shop and people queued down the street waiting to pick up their coffee.

TREASURY

The Treasury Building is regarded as Australia's finest nineteenth century public building. When it became obvious that the vaults in William Street could not hold all the gold coming from the goldfields, a new building was needed. The 19-year-old architect prodigy J.J. Clark designed this in 1857. The Treasury was built in the Italian Palazzo style and was completed in 1862. It was principally used as an administrative centre and all the colony's accounts were kept here. It also provided offices for the Governor, the Premier, the Treasurer, and the Auditor–General. The basement stored gold bullion and once held as much as £200 million worth of gold. Between 1851 and 1860, Victoria produced 20 million ounces of gold, one third of the world's output. The statue is of Gordon of Khartoum, the famous British General. The original casting stands on the Embankment in London.

Melbourne is a city built on gold and it is fitting that the Old Treasury is today used as a gold museum. Here there are two permanent exhibitions. "Built on Gold", located in eight of the old basement vaults talks about the gold fields, the gold escorts, the gold market and the gold rush. "Growing up in the Treasury" recounts the story of life in the building in the 1920s when the Maynards lived there. There is also a rotating programme of temporary exhibitions. Function and meeting rooms are also available to the public. The Old Treasury still performs an administrative function. It is here that the Governor of Victoria comes weekly to meet with the Executive Council to sign off legislation.

The first European settlers travelled up the Yarra in 1835 and by 1837 there was already a population of over 5000 people. Most of the early settlement was around this port area and markets were set up to accommodate the daily commerce of the town. The food that was sold was either produced in the new settlement or brought in by ship. In answer to public demands, a Market Commission was established in 1842 to organise the movement of goods and a general market, later known as Western Market, was built behind the Customs House. It became a wholesale, "cased market" and lasted 90 years. Eventually the Victoria Market in Elizabeth Street on the northern edge of the city absorbed both it and the Eastern Market.

The AXA Building occupies much of the area that was the Western Market, demolished in 1960. The 20-storey AXA building opened in 1965, and, like others built during this time, is unremarkable except for the large public open area in the front which has a water feature and bronze figures of both Batman and Fawkner, reminding us of the historical significance of the place. It was here that Batman was supposed to have said, "This is the place for a village".

Batman sailed on the sloop *Rebecca* from Tasmania in search of pastoral land to add to the 7000 acres he already had in Tasmania. The building at the corner of Market and Collins Street, largely obscured by the trees on the left, is where Fawkner started the first newspaper in 1838. He was also a publican, baker, bookseller, timber merchant, Member of Parliament and bush-lawyer.

In 1837, two years after the first settlement by Batman and Fawkner, the land on which the Mitre Tavern stands was bought for £136. In 1839, a two-storey house was erected on a small section of the original holding. In 1868, the residence was sold and became a public house, licensed to sell alcohol. It quickly became a favourite starting point for local groups hunting the imported deer and a meeting place of the Melbourne Polo Club. Sir

Redmond Barry, the judge who sentenced bushranger Ned Kelly to death, drank here. The original dwelling was bluestone (basalt) and mud-bricks but it was substantially altered to the Queen Anne style about 1900. With its small windows, sharp gables, steeply pitched roof, dark rooms and large fireplaces, it already looked like an English pub. The clientele in the 1920s and 1930s were mainly those who worked in the western section of the city.

The Mitre Tavern is one of the few surviving licensed premises of the early days. Today it is a treasure completely hidden amongst the high towers of the commercial, financial and legal heart of the city. Some of its patrons would like it to remain a secret. Its present owners have been hoteliers for more than 60 years and they have carefully recreated the cosy atmosphere of an authentic English pub, with nooks, booths and alcoves. The plasma television screens and jukebox music might seem incongruous and the local ale of yesterday is now a full range of chilled local and imported beers. The food, too, is international. The clientele are no longer dressed in hunting pinks or navy singlets but it is still a favourite watering hole for many Melburnians, particularly the young, pinstriped lawyers and stockbrokers from the nearby offices.

In this western section of Collins Street, the Olderfleet and Rialto Buildings are extravagant examples of William Pitt's Victorian Gothic architecture. The Woolbrokers' Association and other wool merchandisers originally tenanted the Olderfleet building, constructed between 1888 and 1889, on the site of the first meeting place of Melbourne's Roman Catholics. A little further west was the Rialto Building, so called because Pitt modelled it after the business section of Venice. This ornate building, with its decorative façade, was built for Patrick McGaughan, who was almost as flamboyant as his buildings. The leasehold offices were arranged off an internal gallery and the horses and drays clattered down the laneway between the buildings. As shipping was moving further downstream to the new Victoria Docks, the wool storage areas were used for offices.

Today, the pale green glass façade of the 55 storey Rialto Towers (built in the 1980s) overshadows the intricate rooflines of the Olderfleet and Rialto Buildings. It is hard to imagine that when the original buildings were constructed, they were amongst the tallest in the town. During the twentieth century the buildings had some interesting tenants; the Russian Consul, the Premier Thomas Bent and the Australian Broadcasting Commission.

Commercial and legal firms are now the Olderfleet Buildings' tenants and Le Meridien Hotel occupies the Rialto Building. The stained glass windows, wrought-iron balustrades and cobblestone laneways have been restored and are part of the hotel. Visitors can enjoy fine dining or a business lunch, resting their feet in the grooves worn by drays and horse-drawn vehicles of yesteryear.

During the 1880s some of Melbourne's finest buildings were erected. The Temperance Movement was strong and coffee palaces like The Grand in Spring Street and the Federal Coffee Palace in King Street dominated parts of Melbourne's skyline. The seven storeys high Federal Coffee Palace had a tower topped by a dome 50 metres (165 feet) high. Ships could easily see it as they approached the port. The first two floors had a dining room that could seat 600 people, while the top five floors had many bedrooms. There were six lifts, 7 kilometres (4.4 miles) of bell-wire for electric service bells, eight kilometres (5 miles) of gas piping, fire hoses on each floor, more than five million bricks, and an ice-making plant in the basement. It cost £154,000 to build. By the 1920s the Temperance Movement was declining and the renamed Federal Hotel was licensed to sell alcohol in 1923.

Between the late 1950s and the early 1970s the city began to grow upwards. The idea of a uniform height limit was replaced by a "plot-ratio" formula that encouraged tall buildings with open space at ground level. In fact many did not fulfil the open ground ideal and land speculation in the 1960s and 1970s led to the growth of many uninspiring office buildings crowded together. Community alarm at the demolition of the older city buildings was often expressed too late, struggled for publicity, or was overruled by the authorities. Hence the city lost the Federal Coffee Palace, demolished in 1973. In the mid-1970s the Historic Buildings Preservation Council was formed and listed city buildings to protect them from demolition. Today, this site is a government building, 22 storeys high, housing the Department of Human Services, and formerly accommodating the Superannuation Board.

Bourke Street and General Post Office, Melbourne

There were more than 1000 tree stumps in the eastern end of Bourke Street in 1845 but the section of Bourke Street between Swanston and Elizabeth Streets had stores and hotels where coaches lined up outside the Cornwall Arms and the Albion Hotel to take hopefuls to the goldfields. This was the place to spend money. There were pubs, music halls, coffee palaces and theatres, drunks, prostitutes and thieves. In 1869, Royal Arcade opened, the first of the small arcades that ran between Bourke and Collins Streets. By 1890 Bourke Street was the retail hub of the town with stores like the Beehive Clothing Company, Myer, Coles Book Arcade, the Leviathan, and Buckley and Nunn's. The Melba Theatre opened in 1911 as a picture theatre. It had formerly been The Colosseum in 1868, the Victoria Hall in 1882, and The Queen's Hall around the beginning of the twentieth century.

Today Bourke Street is still the retail hub of Melbourne. However, there have been many changes to the streetscape in the last 80 years. On the right hand side Myer bought all the buildings between its original store and the G.P.O. in 1927 and began to build its empire. Only the name remains on The Leviathan. On the left, the famous Coles Book Arcade became G.J. Coles' Large Variety Store. Rebuilt in 1928–1930, among the first Art Deco buildings in the city, it is classified category "B" by the National Trust, and must be preserved. This store became David Jones' second store. Royal Arcade is much the same, its small stores beautifully restored to their former glory. This section of Bourke Street became a pedestrian mall in 1972, opened officially in 1983 by Prince Charles and Princess Diana.

This modest drapery store was the first Melbourne store owned by Sidney Myer. He came from Tsarist Russia in 1878 and worked in Flinders Lane before joining his brother in the gold mining town of Bendigo. After a few years of successful trading as "Bendigo's busiest drapers", he bought the drapery business of Wright and Neil in Bourke Street for £91,450. Myer introduced a new way of marketing and merchandising to Bourke Street.

Myer's plan was to use this building as the first stage of his model store, an eight-storey steel-framed concrete building. Meanwhile, Myer was purchasing the property that stood between his store and the General Post Office on the corner of Elizabeth and Bourke Street. While construction was being carried out, Myer moved his business to Flinders Street, providing a free bus from Bourke to Flinders to ensure an uninterrupted flow of customers.

The eight-storey Myer Emporium opened in 1913 and was built in the style of the Emporium in San Francisco. The architects were H.W. & F.B. Tomkins and they were to design the later Myer extensions that stretched across two city blocks. The commercial Gothic style appearance of the Bourke Street façade was completed in 1933 and the building made Myer one of the largest department stores in the world. Inside the store is the Mural Room, featuring "Females through the Ages" by artist Napier Waller. Each Christmas since 1956, the seven Myer Bourke Street windows are decorated with scenes appropriate to the Christmas season as a gift to the families and children of Melbourne. Visiting them is a Melbourne institution. Myer has dominated retailing in this area since the 1920s, hence the slogan "Myer is Melbourne". Today it has 61 stores nationally and employs approximately 25,000 people.

The mythical giants Gog and Magog, replicas of the figures in London's Guildhall, stand guard alongside the clock at the end of Australia's oldest arcade, in the oldest retail building in the city. Charles Webb, the architect who was to design the Windsor Hotel in Melbourne, modelled Royal Arcade on arcades in Paris and London. It was a long row of shops, each with elegant bow-fronted windows. Light came from the high glass roof that was decorated with delicate wrought-iron and coloured fanlights. Opening in 1870, it provided a refined atmosphere in which the ladies of Melbourne could shop, away from the dirt, noise and nuisance encountered on Collins or Bourke Streets. The land on which Royal Arcade was built was first purchased in 1837 and then sold in 1855 to Joseph Staunton for £650. It remained in the Staunton and Spensely families until sold in 1958 for £541,000.

Over the years, the Royal Arcade has undergone changes. In 1902 an annexe led to Elizabeth Street, the design mirroring that of the original arcade. The shop fronts, too, have changed over the years and in 2002 and 2003, the original shop fronts were fully restored. Today Royal Arcade remains an elegant corner of Melbourne. Its speciality shops offer a wide variety of goods for the discerning shopper. Customers can purchase silk clothing, fine modern and antique jewellery, gifts from Russia, cosmetics and perfume from France, then relax in the Belgian chocolate shop. At its southern end Gog and Magog (inset) still strike the hours.

Three years after settlement, the first postmaster was appointed, but it was another four years before the first General Post Office (GPO) was erected. The citizens raised money for the clock but the clock hardly ever showed the correct time. By 1859 the first GPO built on the corner of Bourke and Elizabeth Streets had been erected. A grander, two-storey building was built between 1859 and 1867 at a cost of £140,000. This Renaissance Revival building with its columns and high, arched windows had an addition of another storey and a large clock tower added in 1887. It was a huge structure, and was dominant in Elizabeth Street. It was one of Melbourne's exceptional nineteenth century buildings. The GPO was the place from which all distances in Victoria were measured.

Walter Burley Griffin completed the building of the General Post Office in 1919, opening the sorting hall. He was an architect from California who was to be involved in the design of many Australian buildings and became the architect of the new capital, Canberra. The GPO has always been important to Melburnians. This has been a meeting point, just as Flinders Street Station is, and this is where many ring in the New Year. The public viewed with regret the decision of Australia Post to stop using the building as a postal facility in 1992. Various plans were advanced for its future use but finally, in 2001, Schwarz and Garrison won the right to develop the building as a shopping centre. In the same year it was gutted by fire and Melbourne despaired. Plans still went ahead and in 2004 it opened as a boutique-clothing arcade.

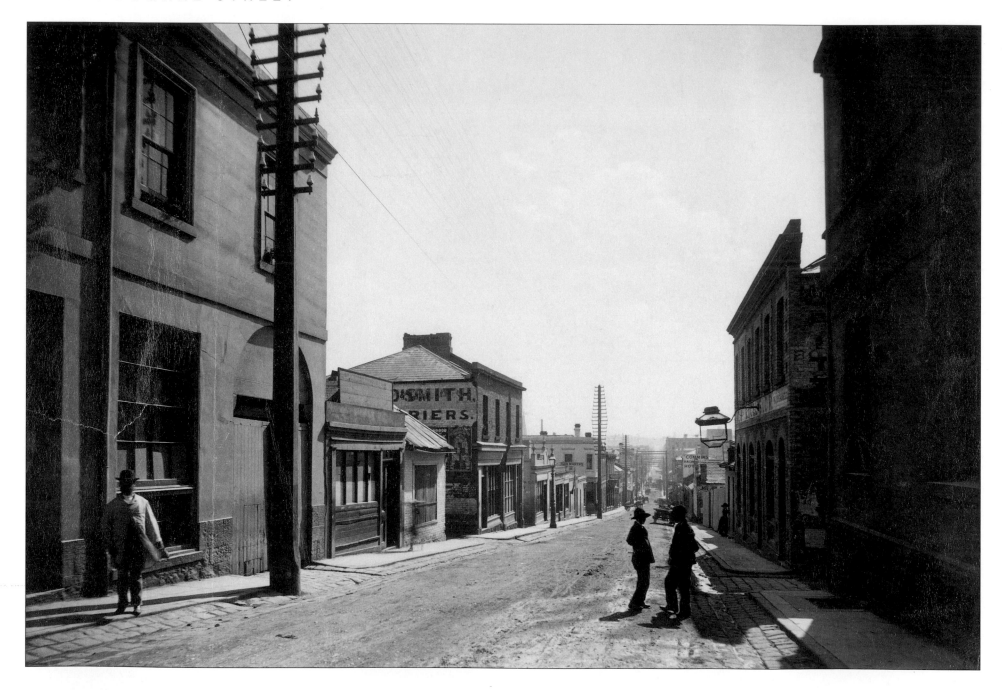

The discovery of gold in 1851 brought large numbers of Chinese to Victoria, just as it had to California in 1848. Some settled in Little Bourke Street, probably because it was on the borders of the town and the land was cheap. Few Europeans ventured into what they considered an alien place of strange smells and stranger sights, an area of gambling and opium dens, bars and prostitutes. Chinese en route to the goldfields bought their provisions and stayed in boarding houses here. Gradually the area began to prosper. Successful businesses such as laundries, furniture and cabinet making flourished. Chinese community associations bought land in Little Bourke Street and Chinatown grew until the early twentieth century. New labour laws at the time decreed that furniture be stamped "European Labour Only". This meant that many would not buy furniture manufactured in this street.

The new century did not bring great cheer for the Chinese in Melbourne. The Immigration Act of 1901 prevented many Chinese from bringing their families to Australia and many in China from coming to this land. It was a land of opportunity only if you looked European and could speak the language. The Chinese population and the numbers of businesses in Little Bourke Street declined. In 1947, with the easing of immigration restrictions, the area again prospered. Restaurants and eating houses of all sorts opened and the street became a focus for all Melburnians in a more cosmopolitan city. Today, it is the heartland of the Melbourne Chinese community. Here their culture is celebrated in festivals, the Chinese Museum, innumerable restaurants and everyday life. The Chinese gateway near the museum is a 1985 replica of the Ling Xing Gate of the Facing Heaven Palace in Nanjing.

Sir Redmond Barry, the famous judge who presided over the trials of Ned Kelly and the Eureka rebels, wanted a library that would be a "great emporium of learning" for all. In 1853 Governor La Trobe granted £13,000 for the building of a library and the purchase of books. In 1856 the Public Library opened with 3,846 books. By 1859, the collection had grown to 13,000 volumes and by the 1870s, to 80,000. Admission was free to everyone over 14 years of age who had clean hands and a respectable appearance. The library closed on Sundays and had limited accessibility for many workers. In 1859, the Travelling Libraries Scheme started distributing books. For a long time the library shared its buildings with the Museum of Art and the Industrial and Technology Museum. The 1890s economic downturn meant that no new books were purchased and many library workers lost their jobs.

Today, the most strikingly different feature of the State Library of Victoria is the addition, in 1913, of the huge domed La Trobe Reading Room with its high skylights. Famous authors have found inspiration here. By 1931 the library had more that half a million books, and after World War II ended there was a great upsurge in readers. The library needed more space, and new wings were added, which were in keeping with the original building. The gallery and the museum that had shared the building for years both moved to other locations by 1999 and the vacated premises are now undergoing renovation. The collection now has more than two million books. The oldest book in the collection is a tenth century manuscript; the oldest item a cuneiform tablet from 2050 B.C., and the most valuable book Audubon's *Birds of America*, worth five million dollars.

Coop's Shot Tower was built in La Trobe Street between 1889 and 1890, a little west of the Swanston Street corner where the Public Library stands. The tower, built from fire-furnace bricks, reached 50 metres (164 feet) and was six metres (20 feet) higher than the city's height limit. There are 327 steps to the top and a rail ladder for part of the ascent. It produced shotgun pellets (shot) when metal was poured through holes at the top of the tower. As they fell through space they formed spherical pellets that then cooled in the metre deep tank of water at the bottom. From here they were shovelled, dried and sorted. Any imperfect shot was re-smelted and returned to the process. Each week more than six tons of lead shot was produced, most to be used as ammunition cartridges. As Melbourne grew around the shot tower, the demand for shot dwindled.

A new retail complex, Melbourne Central, was to be built here, but the Coop's Shot Tower posed a problem. Production of lead shot had ceased in 1960 but the building, which had been part of the streetscape for 100 years, was the oldest of its type in Victoria and had been classified by the National Trust. The solution was to enclose the Tower in a cone-shaped glass dome. The largest glass structure of its type in the world, it is 20 storeys high, weighs 490 tonnes, and has 924 glass panes cleaned by a specially designed mechanical system. Near the Shot Tower, is a Seiko fob watch. Each hour the bottom of the watch drops and mechanical cockatoos, parrots and koalas appear. Two minstrels appear to entertain shoppers with traditional Australian folk songs. Melbourne Central opened in 1991. This complex, spread over two city blocks, has 160 shops, restaurants, a car park, a 55-storey office tower and an underground rail station.

The State Theatre in Flinders Street was the largest picture palace to be built in Australia. Union Theatres were building five atmospheric theatres and this one, built in 1928, supposedly had 4,000 seats but actually had only 3,371. It completely dwarfed the Duke of Wellington Hotel, the longest continuously operating pub in Melbourne, on the adjacent corner. The extravagant Moorish exterior was reflected in an even more lavish interior where stars twinkled on a great blue, barrel-vaulted ceiling, across which clouds drifted—a trick of innovative lighting. Statues, pergolas, pencil pines, doves in flight, and trailing vines ornamented the interior. The Wurlitzer organ cost £25,000 and was transported from the wharves on seven lorries, bringing the city to a standstill. The owners were fined by the City Council but the public interest in this "palace of dreams" was enormous.

During the 1960s the State Theatre underwent changes. Its huge theatre was divided into two smaller theatres, the Forum with 944 seats, and the Rapallo with 627 seats. The former solo organ chamber became a milk bar and the organ was offered for sale, finding a home with the City of Moorabbin. Throughout the 1970s the organ was used for popular concerts, broadcast by the A.B.C. In 1981 both theatres were renamed—Forum 1 and Forum 2—until they closed to the public in 1986. After this they were used for various purposes, and as a Christian Revivalist Centre. The theatre was restored in the 1990s and has since become a heritage attraction. The tiny Duke of Wellington Hotel still functions as a worker's pub and is completely overwhelmed by the backdrop of towering glass and steel structures. But the Moorish architecture of the Forum cannot be overshadowed.

Parliament House, the seat of the Victorian State Parliament, is the most imposing of Melbourne's public buildings. Built from 1855–1892, it was an expression of the wealth and optimism of the colony. Wide steps lead to an imposing Doric colonnade topped with sculpted allegorical figures. Surveyor Hoddle thought it more suitable for a gaol or a lunatic asylum: it does have a dungeon and gun turrets. The Commonwealth Government sat here until it moved to Canberra in 1927. To have a seat in parliament it was necessary to own land worth £2000. To vote you had to either own land worth £50 or be a respectable person. After the Eureka Uprising this changed and by 1857 there were secret ballots and universal manhood suffrage. The steps of Parliament were a place of protest. Stone-makers protested here and in 1856 secured the first eight-hour working day in the world.

Parliament House was originally designed with a north and south wing and a tall dome. From time to time it is still suggested that the dome be built, but with the cost estimated in 2000 to be about $4 billion, it is unlikely that it will ever be constructed. Much money has been spent on refurbishing the interiors. Current politicians at times complain of overcrowding, as all cannot be accommodated in the building. Being a landowner or a "member of a respectable profession" is no longer a prerequisite to having a seat in parliament. The dungeon still exists and is used as a cleaners' tea-room. The escape tunnel, which leads to a picnic shelter in the grounds, is still there, but there is no record that it has been used. Parliament House continues to be a focus for protestors and occasionally the steps accommodate protesting citizens bringing messages to their elected representatives.

This cottage was the home of the parents of Captain James Cook and it was originally situated in the Yorkshire village of Great Ayton. James senior and Grace Cook moved into the cottage in 1755 and their initials JGC 1755 are to be seen above the door. It seems likely that their son, Captain Cook, spent time in it when he returned from the 1770 voyage that brought him to Australia. The cottage was put up for sale in 1933 but the owner didn't want it to go overseas. She eventually relented because she believed Australia was still "in the Empire". Russell Grimwade purchased it for £800 as a gift to the people of Victoria. He wanted it to be a reminder of the humble beginnings of this great navigator, so much a part of Australia's history. It came to Australia in 253 packing cases and was reconstructed in April 1934 in the Fitzroy Gardens.

The ivy-clad cottage has attracted large numbers of visitors over the years. It has undergone two restorations, in the 1950s and in 1978, with great care being taken to make the cottage reflect the eighteenth century. The interior is furnished in a style typical of the mid-1700s and the memorabilia displayed gives us a small idea of life at the time. Outside there is an elaborate cottage garden and a hawthorn hedge surrounds the building. In 1970 it was the scene of protests by local aboriginal groups who reminded people that Cook's voyage to Australia brought dispossession for their people. Today it is one of Melbourne's most visited tourist attractions and a favourite location for garden weddings.

Spring Street and Grand Hotel, Melbourne

Melbourne's great nineteenth century hotel was The Grand. It was designed by Charles Webb, built for merchant George Nipper and opened in 1883. The Grand was built in two stages: the southern half in 1884 and the northern half in 1888, the year of the International Exhibition. It was an impressive building with its many arched balconies and its mansard towers. It was equipped with an intercom system and electric bells, had a magnificent spiral staircase, and a grand dining room where meals were served with full silver service. In the late 1880s James Munro of the Temperance Party bought The Grand. He is said to have set alight his hotel liquor licence then changed the name to The Grand Coffee Palace. George V, as the Duke of Cornwall, and Edward VIII, as Prince of Wales, stayed here. Part of the Australian Constitution was drafted in The Grand.

In 1920, following a visit from the Duke of Windsor, the hotel was renamed The Windsor Hotel and its liquor licence was restored. During the Depression, the hotel maintained its air of sophistication and its clientele remained the social elite of Melbourne. In 1980 Oberoi International Hotels took over the hotel and extensive restoration commenced. The results of this restoration can be seen in the beautiful Grand Ballroom, formerly the dining room, where the huge ornate chandeliers were reproduced from photographs. The entire hotel has been painted in its original colours. Many famous people such as Lauren Bacall, Mohammed Ali, and Omar Shariff have stayed here and many more have enjoyed the Windsor's traditional afternoon teas served on the finest bone china. Liveried doormen dressed in green tails and top hats still greet the guests to this sumptuous hotel.

Princess Theatre. Melbourne.

There is said to be a resident ghost at the Princess Theatre. Opera singer Federici (aka Frederick Baker) died as he descended into the gates of hell in the opera *Faust* in 1888. The Princess Theatre was built to match the grandeur and flamboyance of two nearby buildings: the Grand Hotel and the State Parliament. The style was French Baroque and the first theatre, Astley's Amphitheatre, opened in 1854. Lola Montez, "the miner's darling", performed her seductive "spider dance" there. The present theatre, designed by William Pitt, opened in 1886 with the Australian premiere of *The Mikado*. There is an urban myth that the chorus girls would appear at the Princess Theatre then move quickly across the lane at the back to reappear at the Palace Theatre. The Princess Theatre, with its marble staircase and electric lighting, had the world's first retractable roof.

Renovations in the 1920s destroyed much of the glamour of the Princess Theatre. In 1987, however, David Marriner purchased the building and began an extensive renovation with Allom Lovell and Associates restoring the Princess to its former glory. The theatre was host to the Melbourne production of *The Phantom of the Opera* which required an enormous stage area. Surrounded by more recent buildings, the Princess still retains the charm of the past and has become one of the most important theatres in Melbourne. The big musicals often choose this venue for their productions. Inside the theatre is Federici's bar, named after the ghost. It is said that they used to leave a seat for Federici in the balcony on opening nights. The Princess Theatre is listed on the Historic Buildings Register.

St. James Old Cathedral is Melbourne's oldest original building and dates from 1839, only four years after European settlement. It was first built near the corner of Collins and William Streets in the Colonial Georgian style. Made of bluestone and sandstone, it had a tower topped with a dome rather than a spire. The tower housed eight bells. The first six were hung in 1853, and the two smaller bells in 1885. The interior seating consisted of boxed pews that were originally numbered for rental. Pew number 10 was occupied by the pioneering Henty family. St. James became a cathedral in 1848. The unusual side galleries were for the Governor and the Chief Justice. The baptismal font, probably of the seventeenth century, came from St. Katherine's Abbey on the banks of the Thames, when the Abbey was demolished in 1837. Queen Victoria had to give permission for it to be brought to Victoria.

Today the cathedral is in a different location. In 1913 the rising land values in the central city and the high cost of maintenance helped to convince the church authorities that a move was necessary so, stone by numbered stone, the cathedral was demolished and reconstructed on the site opposite the Flagstaff Gardens (Burial Hill) in King Street. The cathedral entrance moved to face King Street, making its orientation now north/south rather than the original east/west. It reopened for worship in April 1914. Worshippers come from all over Melbourne, but many have a link to West Melbourne, which is no longer a residential area. It became an industrial and then a commercial area. Today, the cathedral fulfils its normal functions and is also used for special services and weddings.

In the late 1800s in Melbourne, firefighting was carried out by volunteers. They were disorganised groups and intense rivalry existed between brigades with frequent clashes occurring. On at least one occasion they turned the water on each other rather than on the fire. In 1890, following the deaths of a number of firemen and the destruction of several buildings, The Fire Brigade Act was passed and the 56 volunteer brigades in Melbourne were disbanded. The Metropolitan Fire Brigade was formed in 1891 and in 1893 the brigade moved into its Eastern Hill Headquarters seen in this photograph. Smith & Johnson designed the building, borrowing elements from a number of sources and it represented state-of-the-art-technology with its 52-metre (169-feet) high watch-tower. There were 59 permanent fire fighters each paid £100 per year, and 229 auxiliary fire fighters retained at 16 shillings per week.

The Eastern Hill Fire Station, which carries a National Trust classification, was the headquarters of the Metropolitan Fire Brigade. Until the 1960s, training for fire fighters involved them turning up at the Eastern Hill Station on a nominated date and joining the "Drill Squad". In 1950 the volunteers were disbanded and fire fighting became a full time career. With the increase in the number and types of fires and the expansion in the duties of the Fire Brigade, the Eastern Hill station could no longer cope with the training of recruits. In 1979, the old head office of the Melbourne Fire Brigade became the Fire Services Museum of Victoria. There are more than 4000 national and international articles related to fire kept there. In a special display run weekly, the East Melbourne Station, next door, shows visitors the work of the fire fighters.

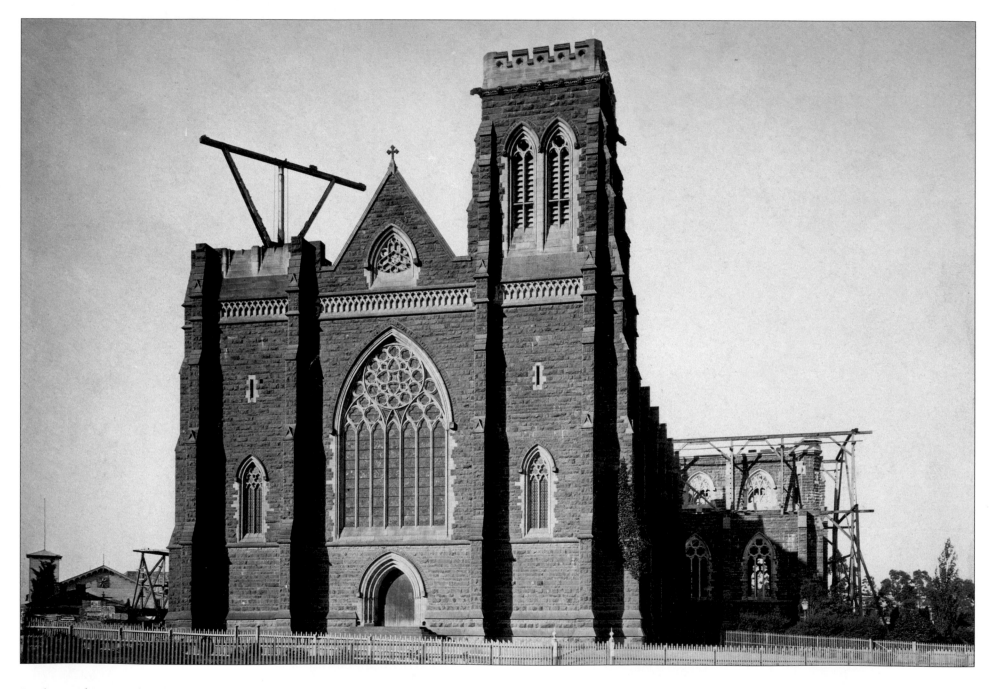

In the opulence and extravagance of the 1850s, the largest church in Victoria, the principal Catholic church in the state and possibly the largest cathedral in Australia, was built. Designed by the English architect William Wardell, one of the principal architects in the colonies at the time, it was started in 1858. It took almost 80 years to complete with its spires—27 metres (90 feet) higher than Wardell's design—being added in 1937 to 1939.

This bluestone building is considered to be one of the finest examples of a Gothic Revival cathedral in the world. While the outside is austere, the interior is flooded with light and the nave features beautiful stained glass by Hardman and Mayer. The Republic of Ireland donated the bronze cross and the interior has a huge open timbered ceiling with carved angels on it. The first Mass was celebrated on the site in February 1858.

St. Patrick's has been favourably compared to the most significant cathedrals in the world, and in July 1972, Pope Paul VI conferred on it the title of Minor Basilica. During his papal visit in 1986, Pope John Paul II addressed the clergy in the cathedral. St. Patrick's once dominated the skyline, but recent skyscraper construction has reduced its prominence. In the 1990s, extensive renovations costing $10 million were carried out. The Pilgrim's Path, the entrance used by most visitors, was designed to evoke a spiritual response and its central concept is flowing water. Aboriginal people have been recognised with the inclusion of a message stick in the cathedral and the stone inlay in the forecourt. The present cathedral choir was founded in 1939, when the Vienna Boys' Choir was stranded in Australia at the onset of World War II.

In 1856, Victorian workers won the first eight-hour working day in the world. Since then, this has been celebrated by the Labour Day holiday in March each year. During the 1880s the Victorian Government granted Crown land for the building of a trades hall and literary institute. Construction began on the Trades Hall Council in 1873. The design was by Reed & Barnes and took over 50 years to complete. Reed & Barnes were also responsible for the

Exhibition Building and Ripponlea. Care was taken to use local materials and it was clear by 1888 that this building with its impressive Corinthian portico was intended for greater things. Indeed it became known as "the working man's parliament". The artisans' school that continued in the new building from 1874, included as students, Tom Roberts and Fredrick McCubbin, who went on to become famous Australian artists.

The Victorian Trades Hall building is one of the oldest union buildings still in use in the world. In 1917 the new ballroom was built for union dances and once was the home studio of Radio 3KZ. A modern multi-storey extension was added in 1961. By the early 1990s, though, the Melbourne Trades Hall had grown quiet, as many long time union tenants had ceased business, or moved to better headquarters closer in to the CBD. The decision was made to make part of the Trades Hall an alternative arts and cultural precinct. In 1996, Trades Hall Council spent $90,000 to replaster and install stage lighting in the New Ballroom. It became a theatre, a ballroom and hosted several Melbourne Comedy Festival gigs. The Trades Hall building is an outstanding example of nineteenth century craftsmanship and has been included on the Historic Buildings Register.

By 1860 Victoria had over 80,000 alluvial gold miners and by 1861, over half of Australia's population of 1,145,000. In 1869 a proclamation and Order-in-Council was issued to give Melbourne permission to set up a branch of the Royal Mint. The building was designed by J.J. Clarke and built in 1872 and is one of the finest examples of Renaissance Revival architecture in Australia. A central courtyard was formed from the four buildings, one on each boundary. The Mint faced William Street between Little Lonsdale and LaTrobe Streets. The administrative building was constructed of brick on a bluestone base and is thought to be the first public building in Melbourne not built of stone. The Melbourne Mint opened for business of 12 June 1872 and a tonne of gold was coined every week. Initially it was guarded by the military but later the police provided the security.

Following Federation, Australia moved to have its own coinage. In 1916 the Melbourne Mint struck its first threepence, sixpence, shilling and two shilling pieces, all of which carried a small "M" under the date. In 1927 Melbourne produced two million of Australia's first commemorative coin—the Parliament House florin. It also produced Australia's most famous coin, the 1930 penny, while the last sovereigns struck at the Melbourne Mint were dated 1931. In the early 1960s the Australian Commonwealth decided to introduce decimal currency and to establish a Mint in Canberra. This new Mint meant the end for the Melbourne branch. The former Royal Mint was the home for many years of the Marriage Registry and the Royal Historical Society of Victoria but has been leased commercially since 2001.

The Supreme Court of Victoria was established by Victorian legislation in January 1852. The design for the new Supreme Court building was decided by a Public Works competition held in 1872 and the building was completed in 1884. High above the entrance stood the figure of Justice with sword and balance, but without the traditional blindfold. The Court was named in honour of Queen Victoria and opened in 1887, in the Queen's Jubilee year. It was designed to house the Supreme Court, the County Court, the Courts of General Sessions and the Court of Insolvency. Initially, eight courtrooms were provided. Each of the courts except one was on the ground floor and extended up to the first floor. Prisoners were kept in the dungeons and brought up from there to stand in the dock.

The Victoria Law Courts are now referred to as the Supreme Court and over the years, eight further courts have been added to the original eight. With the County Court moving to a different site in 1969, the Supreme Court gained sole occupancy of the original building. Under the dome is the Court Library with more than 100,000 books, funded by government grants and compulsory contributions from entrants to the legal profession. Sir Redmond Barry was instrumental in the establishment of the Law Library which, in its early years, stocked books on a wide range of subjects. The court has also taken over occupation of two buildings close by for the Court of Appeal.

EXHIBITION BUILDING, MELBOURNE

The Royal Exhibition Buildings were designed by Reed & Barnes and built by David Mitchell. They were erected for the 1880 International Exhibition that was attended by one million people. The slate-covered dome was modelled on the cathedral in Florence and the temporary buildings covered more than 20 acres. The first Commonwealth Parliament was opened there by the Duke of Cornwall and York (later King George V) in 1901. There have been a number of attempts to demolish these buildings, but they survived to play an important and varied role in Melbourne life. In 1889 the Grand National Baby Show ended in a riot. In the 1919 influenza epidemic it was a hospital, and from 1901 to 1927 the western annexe housed the State Parliament. At different times, different annexes have housed exhibitions, a ballroom, an army barracks, a migrant camp, examinations, concerts and fêtes.

The hall and the gardens are all that remain of the vast permanent and temporary annexes that were built as part of the Royal Exhibition Buildings. The unattractive extensions of the 1950s and 1960s were demolished in 1999 and the interior repainted in the ornate colour scheme of 1901. Art and flower shows, conferences and trade shows utilise the remaining building and grounds. The Museum of Victoria was built in the car park to the north of the Royal Exhibition Buildings and this modern building, which won the Victorian Architecture Medal in 2001, provides a contrast to the grandeur of the Exhibition buildings. In 2001 the Royal Exhibition Buildings were used to stage a re-enactment of the 1901 opening of the first Commonwealth Parliament. On 1 July, 2004, the Royal Exhibition Building became the first building in Australia to win World Heritage listing.

During the 1850s the common way to have a bath was to heat water and put it in a portable tin bath, or to swim in the Yarra River. Pollution of the Yarra caused a typhoid epidemic with many deaths, but people continued to swim in *and* drink the water. To address this problem, the original City Baths opened in 1860. The baths consisted of male and female, first and second class slipper bathrooms, a public wash house and a swimming pool. It was reported that 79,096 men and 2,950 women enjoyed the facilities in the first year. Lack of maintenance caused the building to close in 1899. In 1903 a red brick and cream stucco building, designed by J.J. Clark, replaced it. It was modelled on nineteenth century English public baths and segregated men and women with separate swimming pools and entrances. The red brick and cream design was known as "blood and bandages".

The City Baths introduced mixed bathing in 1947 and in 1954 it was stated that the 85 bathtubs were used 95,000 times. Attendances increased to over 300,000 with the success of the Australian swimmers at the 1956 Olympic Games. However, attendances declined during the 1970s and consideration was given to demolishing the baths. The Builders Labourers' Federation objected to the moves calling the site "the workers' pool". The City Baths were placed on the register of historic buildings and in 1981, $4 million was spent restoring and renovating the site. Public spas and saunas, a gymnasium, sundeck, café, squash courts, and sports medicine clinic were added and the pools upgraded in time for the opening in 1983. Today the City Baths is a health, fitness and wellness centre and is also used as the backdrop for television productions and photographic shoots.

Melbourne in 1860 thought itself opulent enough to finance a great expedition and, in August of that year, Burke and Wills set out to cross the Australian continent from north to south. They reached the Gulf of Carpentaria but perished in the desert in 1861, on the way home. Such was their popularity that in 1863 the first state funeral was held for them and the city was draped in black. Thousands lined the streets to view the cortege as it passed. In their honour, a bronze statue on a granite plinth was erected in 1865. This statue, by the Australian sculptor Charles Summers, was considered one of his finest works. It stood at the intersection of Collins and Russell streets where the residences in the area reflected the affluence of the doctors, lawyers and merchants. In 1886 it was moved to Spring Street to make way for cable trams and where it would be less of a traffic hindrance.

The Burke and Wills statue resided in Spring Street for almost one hundred years. However, traffic was increasing around Parliament House near the statue and it needed to be moved. Melbourne had wanted a central public place for decades. The decision was made to demolish the 1890s Queen Victoria buildings at the corner of Swanston and Collins streets and develop the region into the city square. It was into this area that the Burke and Wills statue was relocated. However this site became the place for protests, controversy and criticism. In the 1980s, the city square was demolished and a hotel and apartment complex opened in 2001. The Burke and Wills statue remains at the corner of what is a simplified open space.

Melbourne University was founded in 1853, a direct result of the wealth from the gold rushes and the desire to prove its equality with Sydney and its university, which was founded the previous year. Part of the reason for the University was to improve the moral character of the colony's inhabitants. In 1854, the Gothic quadrangle, which is at the heart of the University, was begun. A major feature of this area is the Old Arts Building with its clock tower. In 1855 the professors who were to lead the faculties of Classics and Ancient History, Mathematics, Modern History, Literature and Political Economy and Natural Sciences arrived. Women were admitted to the University in 1881 with the first female graduating in 1883. The University had two major roles: to provide professional training for the more affluent, and to provide a site for research.

In 1855, Melbourne University had only 16 students, all male. In 2004 almost 41,000 students were enrolled, 57% of whom were female. The Faculty of Arts has over 7000 undergraduate and postgraduate students enrolled in 1000 subjects. More than 800 of these students come from 50 overseas countries. After World War II the University of Melbourne became a massive institution that was essentially funded by the Australian Commonwealth. From the 1960s onwards it was one of a number of universities in Melbourne and in the 1980s and 1990s it amalgamated with a number of colleges. In the twenty-first century the University of Melbourne has maintained its pre-eminence among Australian universities.

Spencer Street Station, the most important rail terminal in Victoria, was originally known as Batman's Hill Railway Station after Batman's Hill was selected as the site for a railway terminal in 1856. The public witnessed the first passenger train departing from the terminus to Williamstown in 1859. Although there was recognition within a year of the need for major changes due to increased traffic from the suburbs and Geelong, no substantial changes were wrought until the 1880s. In the early 1880s Spencer Street Railway Station acted as an interstate rail transport hub. The 1888 Royal Exhibition prompted the Victorian railways into tourism promotion, and information and booking booths were set up for visitors who wanted to see more of Victoria.

Undergoing a major redevelopment, costing in excess of $700 million, Victoria's most important intra- and interstate transport terminal is a world-class transport hub with connections to regional centres and facilities for train, tram, taxi and bus passengers. The new building has two towers housing apartments and offices, a plaza, retail and commercial premises. The new development takes up the space of three city blocks and will create the largest undercover concourse in Australia. The towers will soar above a graceful, waveform, open weave metal and glass canopy of enormous proportions. Spencer Street Station will be renamed Southern Cross Station. The design facilitates easy pedestrian access to the new residential Docklands precinct.

VICTORIA MARKET, MELBOURNE.

The car park that belongs to the Queen Victoria Markets was Melbourne's first official cemetery. It opened in 1837 and at that time was on the edge of Melbourne far from most activity. It closed in 1854. Thousands of monuments to the "pioneers" were then relocated to Fawkner Cemetery but thousands still remain. In 1868 the Meat Market which faces Elizabeth Street was built and then in 1877 came a number of open timber sheds for the fruit and vegetables, some of the later sheds occupying part of the former cemetery. This site, shown above, was actually chosen because it contained the least used section of the cemetery. The Queen Victoria Market was opened on 20 March 1878, though markets operated from the site prior to that date. The buildings that were erected in Victoria Street in 1887 have some of Melbourne's best-preserved, nineteenth-century shop windows.

Despite threats to demolish the Queen Victoria Markets in the 1970s they survived and are now on the Historic Buildings Register. It is one of the largest and most intact examples of Melbourne's great nineteenth-century markets. Spread over seven hectares, the markets supply fresh fruit, vegetables, meats, clothing, souvenirs and leather goods. Many of the old sheds remain and customers wander up the various aisles making their choices from all that is available. In the meat and fish market, the sellers call out their prices encouraging those who are thinking of purchasing. There are a number of cafés both on the main streets and inside the markets, and buskers entertain on the street. Known as the Queen Vic Markets they attracted over eight million visitors in 2004.

Ned Kelly, the infamous Australian bushranger, was sentenced to hang by Judge Redmond Barry presiding in the Supreme Court on this site in 1880. The Court of Petty Sessions, as the old Magistrates Court was then named, was designed in the Norman Romanesque revival style by George Austin. Constructed entirely from Australian materials, the building is described by the Heritage Council as an example of the "grim majesty of the law".

In 1859, Russell Street became the new site of the Victorian Police Headquarters. In 1940 Percy Everett, Chief Architect of the Public Works Department, designed an outstanding example of an Art Deco building which became the new Victoria Police Headquarters. Completed in 1943, and constructed of reinforced concrete and cream brick curtain walls, it is a rare example of surviving stepped-geometric New York or Los Angeles architectural skyscraper design.

The Melbourne Magistrates Court relocated to the corner of William and Lonsdale Streets in 1990. The building was purchased by Royal Melbourne University of Technology in 1997 and is preserved as part of a unique heritage precinct that includes the Old Gaol and the Watch Tower. Today the Vice Chancellor's and various other offices are on the ground floor. The stone staircase and interior decoration, dark wood lintels and windows have been retained and signage such as "Court Witnesses" remains on the doors.

The Russell Street Headquarters provided a highly recognized police facility because of the many inter-related policing groups located on one site. In 1977 force command and administration were relocated. In 1986, a female police constable died as a result of burns and injuries incurred from a car bomb explosion outside the Russell Street complex. The complex was closed in 1995 when activities were transferred to the new Police Centre. The building is currently used as apartments.

FLEMINGTON RACECOURSE, MELBOURNE.

Since the 1860s, the first Tuesday in November in Melbourne has been the Melbourne Cup public holiday. In 1861, the horse Archer won the inaugural race, having first walked 530 miles to reach the track. The venue of the Cup is Flemington and there have been races held there every year since 1840. At that time the land was a swamp on the banks of the Maribyrnong. Flemington is the oldest continuing metropolitan racecourse in Australia.

Originally called Melbourne Racecourse, it became known as Flemington in the 1860s, named after a nearby town. The Melbourne Cup was a handicap race run over a two-mile course with 18 horses competing. But the Melbourne Cup is more than this. This photo shows the huge crowds drawn by the premier sporting, fashion and social event of the year. They occupy the public grandstands and other facilities that were built for the racegoers.

In 1924, the Members' Grandstand was built at Flemington and the mounting yard moved in front of it. In 1977, the hill, which was a natural vantage point, was used to build a four-tiered grandstand at a cost of $8.5 million. Unlike the Members' Grandstand, this stand is open to the public and has bookmakers, tote and bars. It is opposite the winning post and so is a popular place to view the races. In the 1990s the mounting yard was doubled in size and there was a rebuilding and modernisation of the Flemington racecourse. The Melbourne Cup is still "the race that stops a nation" and the prize money for the race is almost $5 million. It is an event that combines twenty-four horses from around the world. The associated Spring Racing Carnival is one of the main social events of the year and there are a number of feature races and social functions at this time.

La Trobe Street in 1841 was considered a long way out of town but local residents were concerned with the large gaol they saw being erected. Built of bluestone, it was intended to impress the population and demonstrate that escape was impossible. There were really three gaols built between 1841 and the 1860s. The third, begun in 1852, was based on the designs of the British prison engineer Joshua Jebb, and the Pentonville Model Prison in London. In all there were 135 hangings here, the most notable being that of Ned Kelly. He was imprisoned at the same time as his mother who was held in the next cellblock. In 1880, at the age of 25, Ned Kelly was hanged. He told Sir Redmond Barry, the presiding judge who died two years later, that he would see him in hell. Between 1880 and 1923 the gaol was slowly run down and sections were demolished.

The Old Melbourne Gaol was finally closed in 1929, though it reopened during World War II as a military prison for Australian soldiers who were Absent Without Leave. Later, the Victorian police force used it as a storage depot. The 1860s chapel, courtyard and arched main entry remain as do a number of the tiny cells that open onto Victoria Street. While the prisoners may be gone, quite a few believe that there is evidence of paranormal activity in the gaol. Visitors are able to experience the chilling environment of Victoria's oldest surviving remand prison with day or night tours. The Old Melbourne Gaol is considered to be one of the major tourist attractions in the city and shows how prisoners lived and were punished. The complex contains a number of artefacts such as death masks, cells and instruments of punishment. There is also an exhibition on the "Art of Hanging".

The wealth that gold brought to Victoria in the 1850s funded a number of public buildings and it is at this time that the Kew Lunatic Asylum was built. Designed by the Victorian Public Works Department it was probably the largest asylum constructed in nineteenth century Victoria. The barracks-style building had two prominent side wings. These were for the public or non-paying patients: the left for men and the right for women. Paying patients were housed in the front wings. The front garden was used for therapeutic work for the able-bodied. The treatment of mental illness at this time was thought to be enlightened. Those afflicted could be placed in an asylum and a scientific approach, with medical therapies, strong moral guidance and work would help the patients be cured. Few patients were ever healed and the Kew Asylum did not live up to expectations.

The Kew Asylum has dominated the east Melbourne skyline for more than 100 years. In the 1950s, criticism of the outmoded institutions saw Kew Asylum turned into the Willsmere Mental Hospital where the elderly, suffering from mental or physical problems, could be housed. Despite its new use the building was marked for closure and in 1988 Willsmere ceased operating and the land and grounds were sold to private developers. Still called Willsmere, the 25 acres of grounds is now the location for modern housing. These were completed in 1995 and offer close proximity to schools and golf courses. The view, towards the city, is one of the major selling points.

The first port area, where the city originally developed, was at Queen's Wharf. In time, as this became polluted and inadequate for the needs of the population, private wharves downstream—notably Coles Wharf—were built. Other private wharves began operating at Williamstown and at Sandridge because of the difficulty navigating the swampy downstream sections of the Yarra. By 1886 the Coode Canal improved river flow. In 1892 the West

Melbourne or Victoria Dock (shown here) was opened immediately west of the Spencer Street rail yards, complete with a swinging basin for ships. After the 1890s Depression, the locational advantage of these docks was realized and the Coode Canal was deepened to allow for deep-draught vessels to enter. By the end of the decade, Victoria Docks and the North Wharf section of the Yarra were the most important, being the hub of trade until the 1970s.

In the late 1920s, the building of Spencer Street Bridge spelt the end of many of the nineteenth century river wharves. From the early 1940s the tonnages handled by Victoria Docks and North Wharf grew slowly and then declined in the 1970s. Large ships needed room to manoeuvre and wide aprons of land to store the containers. Much of Victoria Docks was not suitable for modern containerised shipping, consequently new facilities were opened at Webb and

Swanson Docks, making Melbourne Australia's biggest port. For nearly a century Victoria Docks had been the hub of shipping movement in Melbourne but is now being renewed, with its historic features incorporated into the new development. Today Telstra Dome has been built on some of this land and the exciting Docklands development is to be a blend of commercial, residential, leisure and retail activities. In the foreground is the 6-lane Bolte Bridge.

From the top of St. Paul's Cathedral, St. Kilda Road stretches towards the south of the city. The clock tower of Princes Bridge Station looked down on the rail platforms below and hansom cabs lined up waiting along Batman Avenue for passengers from the next train. Over Princes Bridge, past the gardens on the right, was Wirth's Olympia flanked by bookbinding, printing and other industries. This triangle of land had been in public use since 1877 when Cooper and Bailey's American circus pitched its big top. Nearby was an entertainment area where visitors could ride on the "tugalong", go down the water chute, or merely sit sipping tea in the Japanese Tea House. In 1907, Wirth Brothers took over the entire site and opened a new circus hippodrome, a roller-skating rink and leased the original Olympia as a cinema.

In the foreground where Princes Bridge Station once stood, the geometric glass and zinc architecturally adventurous Federation Square, with its plaza of pink Kimberley sandstone, dominates. In the middle distance the spire of the State Theatre marks the former site of Wirth's circus. After fire destroyed Wirth's, the area was used as a car park in the 1950s. In 1959, the architect Roy Grounds designed the National Gallery and Cultural Centre. Three centres of the arts were built between 1960 and 1984; the Concert Hall, the National Gallery and the State Theatre, which was to have a spire of gold webbing, the lower section modelled on a ballerina's tutu. Today the spire is lit by 6,600 metres (21,653 feet) of fibre optic tubing, 14,000 incandescent lamps and neon lighting, glowing and twinkling in ever-changing patterns and colours, a unique nocturnal reminder that this is the cultural heart of the city.

The Melbourne Cricket Ground (MCG) was built in the 1850s when the cricket club was forced from its former site near Spencer Street Railway Station. Australia's first steam train would have passed through the oval there. The MCG was where the first international cricket match was played and this was followed by the first Australia—England Test match in 1877. The first grandstand seated 6000. Over the years a number of different stands were built, financed by the subscriptions from the Melbourne Cricket Club members. (Until 1984 only men were allowed to be members of the MCC.) For the 1956 Olympics, the State Government granted £100,000 towards the building of the Olympic Stand. The MCG was the main venue of Olympic events at this time and set a world record for the most people to attend a baseball match.

The MCG now plays host to cricket and Aussie Rules football games. The huge seating and standing capacity of the MCG allowed 121,000 to view the 1970 football Grand Final between Carlton and Collingwood. MCG facilities are constantly being upgraded and in 1992 the $150 million Southern Stand was built. A long-term contract was drawn up between the State Government, the Australian Football league (AFL) and the Melbourne Cricket Club. The current $430 million redevelopment has seen the removal of a number of stands including the 1956 Olympic stand. The MCG has hosted many famous events: International Cricket (the 1992 World Cup Final), the 1986 visit of Pope John Paul II, and in 2006 will host the Commonwealth Games. Membership of the MCC is popular with a waiting list of more than 150,000.

Queen Victoria was born on 24 May 1819 and ascended the throne in 1837 at the age of 18. During the nineteenth century the name Victoria was given to one of the colonies and this name was retained when the colonies became states within the Commonwealth in 1901. Her name is also present on many streets, buildings, parks and lakes throughout the state. Queen Victoria died in 1901 having been the reigning monarch for 63 years. It was said that her death cast a pall across Australasia and in 1905 the Queen Victoria Memorial Act required that £25,000 be paid from the Consolidated Revenue Fund for the purpose of erecting a memorial to her. The Queen Victoria Gardens in the Domain Parklands contains a marble statue of the queen on an artificial mound overlooking ponds where it would be seen clearly from St. Kilda Road. The statue has a four-sided base depicting Wisdom, Progress, History and Justice.

Domain Parklands comprise a number of parks, reserves and gardens. The Queen Victoria Statue is located in the now well-developed Queen Victoria Gardens with their emphasis on flowering garden beds and manicured lawns. The statue, just one of several statues in the gardens, is on a slightly-elevated rise and overlooks a lily-covered pond. There are roses and flowering shrubs and beds filled with colourful annuals. This area is a favourite meeting and picnic spot. The view from St. Kilda Road has almost gone with the growth of trees, but it provides an imposing view from the nearby Alexandra Avenue. Nearby is the famous floral clock, composed of 7000 bedding plants, which are changed twice yearly. A group of Swiss watchmakers gave this decorative timepiece to Melbourne in 1966.

On Armistice Day—11 November—in 1927, the Governor, Lord Somers, laid the foundation stone in the presence of more than 10,000 people. It was "An Everlasting Tribute from the People of Victoria to the Glory of Achievement and the Nobility of Sacrifice." Built between 1924 and 1937 the crown of the Shrine rises to almost 30 metres (200 feet) and at the time could be seen from most of the suburbs and from Port Phillip Bay. It was built of granite and marble and combined Egyptian and Greek motifs. At the heart of the Shrine is the Stone of Remembrance. This marble stone is sunk below the pavement so that no hands may touch it and it is necessary to bow the head to read the inscription, "Greater love hath no man". At exactly 11am on Armistice Day, a shaft of light illuminates the Stone of Remembrance in the Inner Sanctuary.

The Shrine is a growing monument and other memorials have been added to demonstrate the sacrifices and service of previous generations. The Eternal Flame is part of the World War II memorial; the Remembrance Garden commemorates the post 1945 conflicts. A Visitors' Centre was opened in recent years and provides space for permanent and touring displays, an auditorium, interactive touch-screen kiosks, all designed to better educate visitors about the service and the sacrifice of Victorians in different theatres of conflict. There are a number of ceremonies, but it is best known for the annual Anzac Day and Remembrance Day commemorations. On Anzac Day, 25 April, representatives from all the armed services march down St. Kilda Road to the Shrine. A uniformed guard keeps watch over the Shrine throughout the year.

Government House, the official residence of the Governor of Victoria, is located in the precincts of the Botanical Gardens. It was built in the Italianate style and is one of the finest examples of this type of architecture in Australia. In 1841, land was set apart as the Domain Parkland and included space for the future Government House. In 1870, the decision was made to construct the first purpose-built Government House. Notable designers worked on the building—William Wardell, who was responsible for St. Patrick's Cathedral, J.J. Clarke for the Treasury and P. Kerr for Parliament House. Constructed of cement and render the emphasis was on efficiency and it is in contrast to some of the extravagant buildings of the boom period. It was rumoured that Queen Victoria would not visit because the ballroom was half as big again as the ballroom at Buckingham Palace.

The Governor, who is appointed by the Queen, acts as constitutional head of the state of Victoria and as such, hosts many public functions at Government House. Today, Government House and the Mews are both in immaculate condition and are noticeably intact. The house has retained its grandeur and is one of the largest and most palatial residences in Australia. The grounds have been enhanced with the development of the gardens. Its commanding position means that the house is regularly photographed. The tower can be seen from a number of the inner city suburbs and its extensive grounds from city skyscrapers. The National Trust conducts guided tours through the building and the Governor of Victoria extends an invitation to the public to visit on Australia Day in January.

Station Pier opened in 1854 at Sandridge on the coast and was originally known as Railway Pier. Australia's first railway was built to facilitate the transport of people and goods from the pier to the city of Melbourne, which was three miles away. This was necessary to avoid the expense of offloading ships' cargo and people to smaller boats that could move up the then, very shallow, waters of the Yarra River. Within eight years, the

120-metre (131-yard) pier was extended to 661 metres (723 yards) in length. This was to accommodate the large increase in shipping traffic arriving full to the brim with goods and people associated with the Gold Rush in the 1850s. The pier brought the traders and immigrants to the city and Victoria and the promise of glittering fortunes.

Station Pier today remains an evocative landmark of particular significance to post-World War II immigrants. After a decline in use in the 1930s and 1940s, the halcyon days of Station Pier were rekindled in the 1950s and 1960s. During this period thousands of immigrants, particularly from Italy and Greece, disembarked and made their way into a new life. Recovering from a further twenty-year decline in service, Station Pier now has almost one million passengers a year. At 933 metres (3,061 feet) wharf length, it is capable of berthing the largest cruise liners throughout summer and autumn, and is the terminal for the Tasmania ferry service. The passenger facilities have also undergone major refurbishments. The Pier operates 24 hours a day and has a central roadway which allows cars to be driven directly onto seagoing transport.

In 1934, the State of Victoria was 100 years old. Sir Macpherson Robertson, the Australian businessman and manufacturer of fine chocolates, donated £100,000 to mark the occasion. £40,000 was to be used for the establishment of a girls' high school. He felt that the girls had been unfairly treated when the co-educational Melbourne High School was divided and the State Government purchased and developed a campus at Forrest Hill for the boys.

The Mac.Robertson Girls' High School was the result of an architectural competition won by Norman H. Seabrook and reflected the work of the Dutch architect W.M. Dudok. The building, named after its benefactor, officially opened on 7 November 1934. The school motto became *Potens Sui* (mastery of self). In 1942, the school building was occupied first as the U.S. Army Headquarters then by the R.A.A.F. .

The Mac.Robertson Girls' High School's excellent results have made it one of the top academic schools in the state and many of the ex-students are leaders in the community and in their fields. The school has been extended over the years: the Hall Balcony in the 1960s and the Senior Library in the 1970s. Having been gazetted as a Heritage building in 1982, the building was given a National Trust Classification in 1987. In the 1990s floors were leased in a nearby building before work on the Lakeside Development that included a gymnasium, learning resource centre and lecture theatre was begun. The current enrolment at the school is over 950 and there is a strong extra-curricular programme of music, drama, sport and debating. In 2005, the State Premier attended a symbolic ceremony, restarting the clock, seen in the photo, for the second century of State Education.

The establishment of the Melbourne Continuation School in 1905 was the start of State secondary education in Victoria. The school was co-educational and in 1912 became the Melbourne High School. When the building in which the school was housed was considered unsuitable, the State Government decided to erect a high school for 750 boys on the Forrest Hill site in Prahran. It is not clear what model was used to design the building but it does bear a resemblance to The Grover Cleveland High School in St. Louis, Missouri. The desire was to make an architecturally significant building that would welcome in a new era in Victorian education. The building was located on 12 acres of land, cost £100,000 and was officially opened on 7 June 1928. The new school was renamed Melbourne Boys' High School.

Melbourne Boys' High School is the only State select entry high school for boys in Victoria and has a reputation for academic excellence. During World War II, the school was taken over by the Royal Australian Navy and the education continued on two separate sites. Development of facilities began with a physical education centre that included a heated swimming pool, a library and a junior science wing built from 1960 to 1970. The school has a very active Old Boys' Association which has helped to raise funds to develop the school. In 1992, a new building with pool, gymnasium, music centre and library was completed. In 1995, the 1927 building was refurbished and new facilities allowed the school to increase its enrolment to its current 1300 students. The school has a very strong extra-curricular programme of Army and Air Force Cadets, music, sport and debating.

The building of the Alfred Hospital commenced in 1870, following many years of bitter opposition and obstruction from the management of the Melbourne Hospital. Built on almost 15 acres of reserved land in Prahran, the earliest structures, with their Elizabethan features, characterized the architect Charles Webb's work. The administration and first ward block, known as the West Pavilion facing Fawkner Park was solid two-storey red brick buildings decorated with patterns of contrasting cream brick and surmounted by a tower. Four pavilions were planned to accommodate 240 patients. Built along "Nightingale principles", the large wards had 24 beds with enough windows for natural ventilation. The hospital was named to commemorate the recovery of Prince Alfred Ernest Albert (second son of Queen Victoria) from an attempted assassination at Clontarf, New South Wales in 1868.

The Alfred Hospital has national standing as a leading health service provider, offering every form of medical treatment except obstetrics and paediatrics. There is a staff of 3500 and more than a quarter of a million people are treated annually. In 1969, the original administration building was demolished. A plethora of new, colourful purpose-built structures replaced the red brick pavilions and virtually covered the 15-acre site. One, the nation's busiest trauma service unit, is located to the west of the original pavilion. A helipad built on a bridge over Commercial Road facilitates rapid access of trauma victims directly to the hospital. An infectious diseases research unit has been opened with state-of-the-art offices and laboratories and an 81-bed, statewide short-stay surgery and diagnostic treatment facility for public patients is due for completion in 2007.

Some 40,000 years ago, Albert Park was a series of swamps. In 1864 it was proclaimed a park and named after Queen Victoria's consort, Prince Albert. In 1880 the land was excavated to form a man-made lake and fresh water was pumped from the Yarra in 1890. Various sporting groups obtained permission to set up around the lake with The South Melbourne Cricket Club starting up in 1862. The area was also used as a racing track for horses and buggies and the Albert Park Speedway opened in 1903. Onlookers were protected behind timber barricades at the edge of the dirt track.

Albert Park is a 225 hectare area that is known internationally as the venue for the Australian Grand Prix. Over the years it has been a tip, a camp for army reserves and a recreation reserve. In 1993, the State Government announced that the area would host the Australian Formula One Grand Prix. A major redevelopment of the area occurred at the time. Now the Park is a major sporting and recreation venue and a sanctuary for wildlife. The lake circuit walk is popular with runners, joggers and cyclists. There are also rowing and yacht clubs, the Melbourne Sports and Aquatic Centre, 25 ovals and playing fields, restaurants and an 18-hole public golf course. The Park hosts major activities like fund-raising walks, competitions and will host some events of the 2006 Commonwealth Games.

It was illegal to go swimming in the open sea in the 1850s, which is when the sea baths were designed. The baths, with men and women in separate areas, opened in 1860 and included refreshment rooms, a gymnasium and a 234 x 61 metre (256 x 67 yard) swimming area. Social recognition came with Prince Albert, Queen Victoria's first son, visiting the establishment. The baths were very popular: at one time a banner boasted, "the largest and best swimming baths in the world". Eventually, there were four separate enclosures. The last, in 1903, Hegarty's Royal Gymnasium Baths, was the most exotic with a number of domes overhead and hot sea baths. The front was used as a private dwelling, offices and refreshment room, and the two platforms on either side were 91 metres (300 feet) long. A thousand bathers per week used the baths.

Hegarty's Royal Gymnasium Baths were destroyed by fire in 1926 but in 1931 new spacious baths opened providing lockers for over 1400 people. However, the idea of indoor sea baths was outmoded. The St. Kilda Baths began to deteriorate and in the 1950s the wings of the baths that stretched into the sea were considered unsafe and removed. Also removed were the men's baths and the decorative parapets. The domed café was used for a series of nightclubs, but over a period of time there was violence associated with these. In the 1980s the concrete wings were demolished. This left only the sea baths and they too closed in 1993. In the late 1990s, $55 million was spent upgrading the facilities to include a spa and gymnasium, three-storey car park, 25-metre (82-feet) pool and restaurant. The current St. Kilda Sea Baths is Melbourne's only indoor heated sea-water pool.

In 1911, The Greater J.D. Williams Amusement Company acquired a 10-year lease on land in St. Kilda, in order to build a new amusement park. T.H. Eslick and 20 builders from Coney Island, the world's first Luna Park, designed and constructed Melbourne's Luna Park which opened in 1912. In 1913 more than 439,000 people visited the Park. Eslick's stay in India may have been the inspiration for Mr. Moon and the Mogul/Moorish entrance facade. Eslick also built a roller coaster for The Great Durbar Exhibition of Old Bombay, for the visit of King George V in 1911, and the Scenic Railway reflects this design. More than 70,000 lights illuminated the complex at night adding to the excitement and attraction. Despite its success, Luna Park was forced to close in 1916 because of World War I, only being opened for patriotic events.

Luna Park reopened in 1923 in what is now a major Melbourne tourist precinct. It remained open during World War II but under blackout conditions. Refurbishment occurred in time for Queen Elizabeth II's coronation in 1953 but in the years after, there were few changes made. In 1999 the carousel was renewed at a cost of $2 million, utilizing the skill of 50 people over two years. In 2001 Luna Park itself was closed and $10 million spent on refurbishing the site. The old favourites were retained, new high-speed thrill rides were added along with conference facilities. Luna Park has iconic status in Melbourne and the Scenic Railway is now the only antique roller coaster still operating with brakemen-operated carriages. The slogan, "Just for fun" was and is appropriate for the generations of children and adults who have visited Luna Park.

In 1840 speculators were able to purchase land in the Brighton area for approximately £1 an acre. Henry Dendy, in England, was able to purchase 20 square kilometres (8 square miles) of this land, sight unseen. What was a rustic fishing village soon became a place of fashionable residences with bathing boxes and boatsheds. The first bathing box was believed to have been erected in 1862 without a building permit. By the 1930s approximately 200 licensed bathing boxes extended along the beachfront. However, there was a great deal of dispute regarding the original land titles that had been granted for these boxes. Most of the boxes were built near the water's edge so that the affluent could enter the sea without getting sand between their toes. During the Depression of the 1930s, the 120 scattered bathing boxes were relocated to Dendy Street and in 1934 they were moved back from the high water mark.

Many bathing boxes around the Bay were destroyed by inclement weather and neglect and, from 1970 onwards, removed in response to conservation groups' demands that saw them as foreign to the natural environment. Brighton licensees fought for the retention of their boxes because they were on freehold land owned by the former City of Brighton. The remaining 82 gable-roofed, timber bathing boxes are colourful and part of the tourist attractions of the area. While the boxes can only be used for changing and storage of beach items, they are highly desirable and bring high prices. In 2000 the Brighton bathing boxes were listed on a City of Brighton Planning Scheme Heritage overlay. In 2005 one sold for $156,000. Bathing boxes feature in many aspects of Melbourne life, appearing in bridal photographs, on the cover of telephone directories and in tourist brochures.

The Chapel Street of the 1830s was a bush track that achieved permanent status by the 1840s. It was named after the first chapel, and over the next 20 years, shops and dwellings were erected. In 1886–8 the general store disappeared, replaced by more specialised shops such as the grocers and milliners. At this time, the cable tram was laid on wooden blocks that did occasionally catch fire but everyday, thousands of shoppers and workers used this form of transport. Chapel Street was a pioneer in the move towards strip-shopping and this was because of accessible transport. Read's Store, initially a menswear shop, and seen here with the twin domes, was a landmark building in the area. It was taken over by Charles Moore and the new emporium Charles Read Co. opened in 1903. Opposite was the engine house that housed the machinery to power the cable for the cable trams.

By World War I Chapel Street rivalled The Block in the CBD as the place for fashion and shopping. There were also several theatres and cinemas. Before the 1960s, businesses and hotels were closed by 6pm and it was common to see families with children in pyjamas window-shopping in the evening. Today, Chapel Street is one of the most important strip-shopping areas in Melbourne. Restaurants, cafés and speciality clothing shops make this one of the places to be, particularly for the young and the fashion conscious. The street has more diversity than a shopping mall and it is not uncommon for people to spend the day strolling along the street, taking advantage of what is offered. Read's Store, with its twin domes, is still apparent but has been redesigned to become Pran Central, with speciality shopping on the first and second floors and apartments in the upper levels.

Ripponlea is a 33-room mansion designed by the architect Joseph Reed and was built in the Romanesque style between 1868 and 1887. Its owner was the politician and prominent Melbourne businessman Frederick Thomas Sargood, who had huge warehouses in Flinders Street. He gave the house his mother's maiden name. The house is noted for its conservatory, iron *porte-cochere* and stylistic innovations, and the house grew larger as Sargood grew richer.

Ripponlea recycled its own water to use on the gardens and lake, and the magnificent garden that surrounds Ripponlea is believed to be one of the finest examples of a nineteenth century urban garden. It contained vast lawns, a fernery, flower gardens, a lake with bridges, lookout towers, pavilions and islands. In 1903 Sargood died and in 1904 Sir Thomas Bent acquired the property and disposed of 35 allotments from the estate.

Sir Benjamin Nathan acquired Ripponlea in 1911 and it was kept as a family home until his daughter left it to the National Trust in 1963. The house itself was extended to the size we see in today's photograph. It combined Victorian decoration with the Hollywood lifestyle of its last owner. In the 1940s, Ripponlea was famous for hosting charity functions. Some of the land was sold during this period and in 1954 the Australian

Broadcasting Commission purchased a parcel for its television studio. The National Trust took control of the mansion in 1974 and the public was admitted for the first time to see the home, grounds and life of the wealthy. Upwards of 50,000 people now visit Ripponlea each year. With Melbourne being water conscious, Ripponlea's ability to recycle its own water is being reinstated.

Stonington was built in 1890 as a private residence for John Wagner, who gained much of his wealth from Cobb and Co. Coaches. Charles D'Ebro, the architect selected to design a splendid mansion in the Italian Renaissance style, worked on constructions such as the Princes Bridge, which remain in use today. The Classical style of the house is typical of the late Boom period in Melbourne and the interior has an elaborate great hall and staircase. The roof was made of almost 20,000 roofing slates imported from North Wales and 100kg (220 pounds) of nails were used to fix the roof. The large wrought iron gates and gatehouse posts were imported from England. The grounds were extensive and the garden was considered a showpiece. Stonington served as Victoria's Government House from 1901 to 1931 and the State Government purchased the house in 1928 for $35,000.

Stonington has hosted many famous people. These include the Duke and Duchess of York (King George VI and Queen Elizabeth), Lord Kitchener and the Prince of Wales (Edward VIII). Stonington is also believed to have a ghost: the son of the Earl and Countess of Stradbroke, who died there in 1925. From its beginnings as a grand home and then Government House, Stonington's career has been varied. It became a girls' school in 1931, a Red Cross convalescent hospital in 1939, Victoria's health administrative centre in 1953, a tertiary education centre with the Toorak Teachers College in 1957. In 1992 the Toorak campus was amalgamated with Deakin University and has moved from teaching undergraduates to becoming the University's Melbourne administrative headquarters. Stonington is classified by the National Trust as a building of national significance and the University is undertaking its restoration.

Lygon Street, Carlton.

Greetings from Carlton.

Lygon Street, situated in the suburb of Carlton, is one of the great food precincts of Melbourne. It has its origins in the early immigration of Italians to Melbourne and, in particular, to Carlton. Italian migration to Australia first commenced in the second half of the nineteenth century, during the difficult times after the unification of Italy. When Robert Hoddle, Government Surveyor, came to survey Carlton in 1852, care was taken to lay out streets in an orderly grid. In 1887–8, though tramlines were opened along Elgin, Rathdowne and Nicholson Streets in Carlton, there was no tram along Lygon Street. However, it had substantial rows of shops and commercial buildings. In 1916 the electric tram began in Lygon Street and replaced the horse-drawn buses. By the turn of the century, Carlton was home mostly to artisans, workmen and small industries.

Lygon Street has a bigger selection of Italian restaurants and cafés than anywhere else in Australia, and was the first suburb in Melbourne to promote eating outdoors and tables and chairs on footpaths. It owes much of its growth and popularity as an eating out destination to the students from Melbourne University, who frequented the street long before it became fashionable with business people. Wining, dining, *caffé lattes* and Italian delicacies are a feature of Lygon Street. Every October, Australia's largest street festival, Festa Primavera, celebrates great food and great entertainment. The formation of the Carlton Association in 1969 meant that many of the nineteenth century buildings in Carlton and Lygon Street were saved and thus the character of the area retained.

In the nineteenth century the regular rotation of the earth was the only time standard. An astronomical observatory was thus necessary and after vibration from the new railway made the original site unsuitable, it was decided to move to the Royal Botanical Gardens in 1863. The main building of the new Observatory was designed by Gustav Joachimi and included a library, transit room with north/south roof slits, Prime Vertical Room with two east/west slits, meteorological room and a telescope room. Although the Observatory was close to the city, there was no electric light at that time, so observation of the horizon was not difficult. In 1887, a decision was made in Paris to photograph the entire sky and the Melbourne Observatory was allocated a portion of the sky appropriate to its latitude. The camera used was designed by Thomas Grubb of Dublin and the photographing completed in 1892.

In 1907, the newly-formed Commonwealth of Australia took control of meteorology, so the Observatory lost half its staff. In the 1920s, local radio stations used the Observatory to broadcast time signals, but in World War II most of the work at the Observatory was suspended and in 1944 the Commonwealth Solar Observatory took control of the site which was closed a year later. The Department of Weights and Measures occupied the buildings for the next 50 years. When that department was relocated, The Royal Botanical Gardens refurbished the site. This was completed in 1999 and there is now a bookshop, visitors' centre and a café close to the Observatory. Interpretation displays inside the telescope, the return of the photoheliograph and viewing nights have rekindled public interest in the building.

Tasma Terrace, once comprising seven three-storey buildings, was constructed in two stages. The first three buildings were erected in 1878 for George Nipper, grain merchant and ship owner. He wanted a Melbourne house grand enough to entertain distinguished visitors. The remaining four buildings were designed by Charles Webb in 1886–7 for bookmaker, Joseph Thompson. Thompson never lived there but one of the occupants ran a "Trained Nurses Home". Tasma Terrace is one of the finest terraces in Melbourne and an example of Boom-style terrace architecture. It was built with bluestone foundations, cast-iron lacework and tessellated ceremonial spearheads on the fence railings. The buildings were initially named Parliament Place, but became associated with the name Tasma in 1905 when No. 14 was run as a private hotel. Unfortunately, one of the buildings was demolished in 1940.

The Tasma Terrace precinct has had a variety of uses. It was home to medical suites, Public Works Department Offices and finally became the property of the Crown Lands Department. In 1969 the National Trust was informed that Tasma Terrace was to be demolished and a series of high rise towers built there. Thus began a campaign to save the buildings. Media, organizations, individuals and the National Trust became involved. It was not until 1972 that the Government announced that legislation had been passed, the first of its kind in Australia, called the Government Buildings Advisory Council Act. The Council recommended that Tasma Terrace be preserved and in 1978 Tasma Terrace became the registered headquarters of the National Trust. Tasma Terrace has since been restored as far as possible to its original appearance.